Living
in Sin:

The Victorian
Sexual
Revolution

Living in Sin:

The Victorian Sexual Revolution

Wendell Stacy Johnson

Nelson-Hall Chicago

Library of Congress Cataloging in Publication Data

Johnson, Wendell Stacy
    Living in Sin.

    Bibliography: p.
    Includes index.
    1. Authors, English—19th century—
Biography. 2. Great Britain—Social life
and customs—19th century. 3. Sex customs—
Great Britain—History. 4. Sex in literature.
5. English literature—19th century—History
and criticism. I. Title.
PR 105.J58   820.'9' 353   78-268435
ISBN 0-88229-445-8 (cloth)
ISBN 0-88229-649-3 (paper)

Manufactured in the United States of America

10   9   8   7   6   5   4   3   2   1

For James Maloy

Contents

Preface

The word "Victorian" and the phrase "sexual revolution" may not at first glance seem to belong together. In fact, one seems to contradict the other. In our times, to be Victorian can still mean to be against sex—to be extremely conventional, prudish, sexually repressed, and sexually repressive.

Yet the first widespread attacks upon the conventions of sex and marriage, prudery and hypocrisy, and upon the suppression of one sex—women—occurred in the Victorian Age, between the 1830s and the beginning of the 1900s.

The age, more than any other except our own, was schizophrenic and/or ambivalent about sex.

This was the high point for censorship—when sizable portions of Chaucer and Shakespeare could be considered too indecent to be published—and the point when outright hard-core pornography, for the first time, flooded a popular market. This was the period when the assumption of women's passivity, both

sexual and social, came to be fiercely articulated—and when the
first major assaults were made upon that assumption.

In other words, it was a time of conflict, a time of battle. Or,
more precisely, a time of *battles* about sexuality and sexual roles.

The battles were joined, sometimes willy-nilly, by the artists,
writers, politicians, and other public figures touched on in this
book: John Stuart Mill, the Brownings, George Eliot, Charles
Dickens, Dante Gabriel Rossetti, Algernon Charles Swinburne,
Richard Burton, and the rest. The battles were poignant, sometimes remarkably trivial.

But, in any event, the people involved took it all seriously.
Most of them were aware of being caught up in revolutionary
changes. And that is the reason for the subtitle of this book.

As for the title: just when Sex had come to suggest Sin and
Sin to suggest Sex in the popular mind, there was also a vast reaction—partly underground and partly open—against such a
limited and pseudoreligious definition of human psychobiology.
The phrase "living in sin" was spoken and taken straight by most
(but not all) mid-Victorians. More and more, as the century progressed, it sounded ironic if not comic.

1
The
Century
That
Discovered
Sex

Could you hurt me, sweet lips, though I hurt you?
  Men touch them, and change in a trice
The lilies and languors of virtue
  For the raptures and roses of vice.
(Algernon Swinburne, 1866)

That libertinism of the most demoralizing character flourishes in
London, in Paris, and in New York, cannot be a secret; nor that
it is confined to no grade of society.
(Francis Newman, 1867)

Tell me where are there such blisses
  As the sexes can impart?
When lips join in heavenly kisses,
  When they both convulsive start!
(*The Pearl*, 1879)

Did Queen Victoria have a lover? A good many of her subjects thought so. In 1867, *Tinsley's Magazine* published that rumor, linking the Queen's name with that of her Scots servant John Brown—only, virtuously, to deny that it was so. There were other versions of this story about the royal widow. One was that Victoria had secretly remarried; the irreverent weekly *Punch* went so far as to print a drawing of her with the caption "Mrs. John Brown." London, if not the whole realm, was talking. And her behavior was never calculated to discourage the talk. It hardly helped matters when the crusty Brown was seen speaking familiarly to his mistress and sovereign, or when, having accidentally pricked her while putting on her cape, he was overheard to shout, "Hoots, then, wumman, can ye no hold yurr head up?"

Victoria was no Restoration beauty—and no daring Elizabethan spirit either. If the public speculated so much about the sex life of its aging, dumpy, widowed Queen, what was being said about other people?

The answer involves more than speculation. It involves scandalous behavior, suspected and uncovered, and some scandalously daring opinions about the rights and wrongs of sex. The fact is that Victorian men and women were nearly hypnotized by the very idea of sexuality. Chaucer's fourteenth century had its bawdy tales and seductions. The seventeenth-century court of Charles II represented a time and place inordinately given to sexual intrigue, when every nobleman was expected to have at least one mistress—assuming he was neither a puritan (but they were out of favor, having killed the King's father) nor exclusively homosexual (and the Earl of Rochester, who wrote anti-feminine poems about buggering his page, kept mistresses, too). The eighteenth century of Laurence Sterne, whose novel *Tristram Shandy* refers to genitals and copulation on every page, was hardly a time of universal purity—even though the letter writers of that age seemed sometimes more concerned with bowel movements than with fornication. Yet in each of these periods an interest was displayed in something that was partly different from, and simpler than, what we now mean by sex. Chaucer, Rochester, and Sterne wrote about flirtation and desire, about penises and pudenda, dildoes and diseases, heterosexual intercourse and some variations on it. They did not express what nineteenth-century prudes and pornographers were likely to reveal: a fascination with, and fear of, sexuality as *the* controlling force in the lives of human beings.

The nineteenth century was the first since ancient times that generally regarded sex as a terrifying power, one that could virtually be a religion or replace religion. This obsession with the sexual urge that lay just beneath the Victorian surface—and not always *beneath* it—had a quality and an intensity that were new to the Western world.

Victorian fascination with sex is suggested not only by the incredibly widespread prostitution in England a hundred years ago (the police knew of more than eight thousand prostitutes in London alone), but also by the amount of pornography sold and collected—pornography that included (apparently even more than earlier examples) such taboo aspects as incest, sadism, and masochism, as well as several varieties of homosexuality.

Pornography can sometimes tell more about a country and an age than the essays of historians and sociologists. Victorian dirty pictures, for example, usually reveal not just a lusty interest in sex of all kinds, but an artist's desire to thumb his nose at the sacred cows of his society. (Dirty photographs, incidentally, replaced drawings relatively late in the century, unless one counts the photographs of naked nine- and ten-year-old girls taken by the Reverend Charles Dodgson, the "Lewis Carroll" of *Alice in Wonderland*.) The woman, usually plump, who offers her bare front or rear is almost always pictured pulling up or pulling down masses of clothes and underclothes in which she has been bundled; her male companion may well wear a top hat as well as an erection. A favorite subject was the nun lifting her habit to be penetrated by a priest; the motive was probably less anti-Catholic than anti-institutional. Part of the excitement for Victorian audiences in this kind of pornography, then, was its flouting of social and, specifically, religious rules and forms. The same is true of dirty stories.

In a typical Victorian pornographic tale or novel, a boy of twelve may discover sexual differences by playing with his sister, tickling her between the legs. Then he may seduce, or be seduced by, his buxom Nanny when he accidentally sees her naked buttocks (Victorians seem to have loved ample behinds) and arrange to have her handle him sexually as she tucks him in. Wild and frequent bouts in bed would invariably result. Next, at school (for boys only, of course), he may discover the pleasures of mutual masturbation, of being fellated, and at last of sodomizing younger boys. As a young man, after having been seduced by a few prostitutes and after seducing a number of housemaids, he may meet a debauched older woman and her equally debauched husband—usually titled—and become part of a sex circle that includes various aristocrats, wealthy rakes, perhaps a bishop, and a young manservant with incredible genital endowments, as well as some assorted virgins who are deflowered at their orgies. He may also become friendly with a slightly older man who lusts after young boys (according to nineteenth-century expectations, this homosexual male should have full breasts and a small penis), and then arrange to keep a voluptuous widow occupied—in bed

—while his friend penetrates her pretty son anally. This is a composite story, with elements taken from a number of actual tales; it includes the fantasy adventures most often represented in such writing.

We have to remember that pornographic pictures and, especially, stories like this were popular in Victorian England among all classes. At the same time, the "proper" attitude that most middle-class people expressed in public was horrified disapproval of nude paintings and statues, an insistence that the bawdy parts of Chaucer and Shakespeare be cut out of books, and in general, a refusal to say anything at all straight or simple about sex. Women's legs were "limbs," and they were covered down to and including the ankles. (For that matter, even in sex drawings, and later, in photographs, the sexually exposed woman was likely to have kept on at least her long black stockings and her shoes.)

Thus, Victorian horror of sex—as expressed in prudery, in the expurgation of art, and in the bowdlerizing of books—was much more obvious in polite society than its counterpart, Victorian compulsiveness about sex. But pornography and prudishness, prostitution and preaching against the fornicator, all indicate, in one way or another, an obsessive interest in the subject.

Why should sex as an awful force rather than as a fact of life be so deeply felt in this particular age? The question has usually been asked in a different form: Why were so many Victorians so fearful of anything sexual? And it has usually been answered by reference to the rising middle class. Sometimes historians make it seem as if the middle class, like a particularly yeasty mass of dough, has been constantly rising since the thirteenth century. But it is true that in the middle of the nineteenth century, an evangelical-puritan ethic associated with this overwhelmingly Protestant group came to dominate most of society—that is, to define what could be written, said, and openly done in levels of society from the upper gentry to the respectable working class. Perhaps only the very poor and the very rich were free of such influences, for better or worse. The Queen herself was less a regal figure than a frump in the middle-class style—in spite of all the speculation.

Victorian scholar Walter Houghton gives three further reasons for the nineteenth-century fear of sex in his book *The Victorian Frame of Mind*. First, the new popularity of erotic literature—or what seemed erotic, especially in French novels—made people fear that the effect of general education and the enormous increase in literacy were leading to more widespread whoring. The novels of Honoré de Balzac and George Sand, and later (but worst of all), those of Emile Zola were widely and loudly condemned. Alarmingly, they remained much in demand. The critic Matthew Arnold, who was not known for priggishness, wrote in horror about the goddess of sexual license, the "Goddess of Lubricity": "here is now a whole popular literature . . . at her service! stimulations and suggestions by her and to her meet one in it at every turn!" And this earlier "literature of prostitution" was tame indeed compared to the entirely English pornography of the 1870s and 1880s, which Arnold possibly never saw (although he died in 1888). This later Victorian pornography—not just realistic fiction but the real hard-core material—might have seemed, for an elderly Englishman, an echo of the coarseness of the earlier Regency period. William Makepeace Thackeray, who was born the year the Regency began (and was just nineteen when George IV, the former regent, died) was hardly a Victorian prude. He shocked Charlotte Brontë into rage by taking lightly the sexual looseness of both the novel *Tom Jones* and its creator, Henry Fielding. But Thackeray was revolted by the regent, that worst of all the Georges, who was drunk at his wedding, was openly adulterous, and was contemptuous of his wife. George's pre-Victorian court, at least until 1820 when he was crowned, had been as brutal as it was lewd: seduction was common, sobriety rare. And now, with the flood of sex literature in the latter half of the century, many serious people apparently wondered if England was reverting to the tone of that earlier part of the century. Only now, the debauching of young men and women would not be limited to the aristocracy. These were what Houghton calls "signs that the sexual impulse was threatening to overflow the traditional dykes."

Second, the idea of free love—expounded much earlier by the courageous and redoubtable Mary Wollstonecraft, by her son-in-law Shelley, and by other Romantic radicals—was being openly

practiced in America by followers of utopian socialist Charles
Fourier. Not many Victorians specifically advocated free love in
the sense of complete sexual license. Alfred Tennyson, poet lau-
reate from 1850 until his death in 1892, worried a lot about the
phrase and the idea, especially in *The Idylls of the King*; but he
was finally and decisively on the side of marriage. Of course, not
many Victorians bothered to distinguish unbridled and promis-
cuous sex or "free love"—from, say, George Eliot's living for
years in sexual intimacy with someone else's husband. Again,
there was a sharp distinction in practice between the middle class
and the lower working class; the costermonger and his woman
might live together without scandalizing the neighbors, but if a
gentleman—or a man in trade with gentlemanly pretensions—
resorted to a mistress or a prostitute, he had to do it secretly.
(The pornographic novel *My Secret Life*—which may or may
not really be an autobiography—suggests that the secrecy was
part of the thrill.) Some reformers and radicals spoke out against
this gentlemanly hypocrisy—for one, the early Victorian socialist
Robert Owen. But any such attacks as Owen's against the commercial basis of marriage contracts could be denounced as attempts to undermine the institutions of marriage, the family, and
the state, since it was upon the family that the structure of
national life, and indeed of all civilization, was generally supposed to depend.

Another reason Houghton mentions may make some of the
Victorian horror of uninhibited sex seem less foolish. In an England where, by the middle of the century, middle-class sexual
promiscuity was on the increase, prostitution was a glaringly obvious fact. A French observer of English life, Hippolyte Taine,
commented that in the 1860s, it was impossible to walk a hundred
steps in some of the major London streets without jostling
against twenty harlots.

Of course, Victorian moralists tended to be more concerned
about the sexual purity—or, at least, the venereal health—of
men than they were about the hard lot of women who were lured
or forced into prostitution. The "Remedies for the Great Social
Evil" prescribed by F. W. Newman included banning from
schools those classical works, those "poems, plays, sculptures, and

paintings," that "inflame passion in boys and young men." Newman defended himself against the charge of prudery by exclaim-
ing about the "eight thousand harlots in London alone" and how
"many of us are early and profoundly corrupted"; but the "harlots" were considered only as temptations and the "us" appeared
to be only males!

Yet there were at least some Victorians for whom the "great
social evil" of prostitution also implied the suffering of females.
When he was prime minister, William Gladstone regularly took
prostitutes home to his wife; they were given food and sympathy
along with tracts and moral advice. That may at first seem ridiculous, but when one considers that the exploitation of very
young girls was attested to by all kinds of documents—sociological, pornographic, and moralizing—it was in fact a remarkably humane gesture. Of course, Gladstone's actions could
amount only to a gesture: as a Whig he was not likely to advocate anything like equal wages for women. A clear recognition
that "the evil" was essentially economic came later in the century. In 1894 George Bernard Shaw said flatly (in his Preface to
Mrs. Warren's Profession) that "prostitution is caused, not by female depravity and male licentiousness, but simply by under-
paying, undervaluing, and overworking women."

But perhaps there are still more basic reasons for the Victorians' preoccupation with sex—two in particular.

The great shift from an agricultural to an industrial society
brought about the crowded urban conditions and intermittent
bad times that led to so much prostitution; it also tended to
make casual, or short-term, sexual relations an alternative to
long-term relations with mate, kin, and neighbor. A result was
that—for the working and lower-middle classes, and perhaps increasingly for the middle class as well—sexual intercourse began
to replace the more traditional kind of social intercourse.

However, another reason for the Victorian obsession with
sex may be even more important. We saw that by mid-Victorian
times, the word *sin*—as in the phrase "living in sin"—was likely
to mean one thing only. Of course, traditionally there were
plenty of other sins. And the worst of those so-called deadly sins
was not sexual lust at all but pride. Why, then, should the *con-*

sciousness of sin be fixed almost exclusively on sex? One answer lies in another fact we observed: that sexual passion, more than ever before, offered the greatest competition and the greatest threat to orthodox religious beliefs. (Religion and sex have always been closely related. Most religions began as celebrations of fertility, of human sexual fertility as well as the cyclical fruit-fulness of the land.) Undoubtedly, sexual energy has, throughout history, been channeled into various religious forms. Now, in the nineteenth century, there appeared to be a breakdown of Christian faith among intellectuals, among the poor, even among those respectable people who kept up a facade of piety, of church-going, for social reasons. Although many think of the Victorian period as the last age of true and universal faith, actually it was a time—the first time in the Christian era—when traditional religious faith was widely doubted and denied. As religious belief grew weaker, sheer sexual passion threatened to replace Christianity as the emotional center of men's lives. Algernon Charles Swinburne suggested this possibility in his "Hymn to Proserpine," in which he recreated the pagan attitude toward Christ and the old gods—including Proserpine, the goddess of seasonal fruitfulness—at the beginning of the Christian age. To Swinburne, this goddess implied sexual as well as agricultural meanings. In his imagined speaker's address to the new god—"Thou hast conquered, O pale Galilean; the world has grown grey from thy breath"—he also evoked the Cytherean goddess of sex, called Aphrodite or Venus; and he predicted the death of Christianity.

Less openly and shockingly anti-Christian, Matthew Arnold also dramatized his skepticism about the Christian faith—the turning away from traditional religion, and the turning toward sexual love to replace it. His speaker in "Dover Beach" declares that

> The Sea of Faith
> Was once, too, at the full, and round earth's shore
> Lay like the folds of a bright girdle furled.
> But now I only hear
> Its melancholy, long, withdrawing roar.

And he concludes, "Ah love, let us be true/ To one another!" The Christian sexual bond of marriage has always been considered a sacrament, a symbolic expression of faith in the relationship between God and the soul. But love and marriage, the joining of two people through a sexual union, now became an alternative to that faith. Actually, it became a *replacement* for faith.

Was it all a matter of tracts and poetry, this Victorian obsession with sex? What were the private lives of men and women really like? What were the Victorians actually doing? One might reply, "Just about everything."

Free love, adultery, male homosexuality and (in spite of the Queen's disbelief) lesbianism, nymphetism, sadism and masochism, exhibitionism—the Victorians practiced them all. As we said, the number of whores per acre in mid-Victorian London and the consumption of pornography—from expensive illustrated books of erotica like those in Lord Houghton's vast collection down to cheap popular magazines, with their free use of four-letter words—would put today's Times Square to shame.

Most shocking of all, however, was what some great and famous people were doing and saying: not the "other Victorians" that Steven Marcus wrote about in his book on pornography, but influential Victorians, the celebrated public figures, artists, and intellectuals. We may still think of them as smug and prudish, but these were some of the people who, willy-nilly, anticipated—and in a way, inaugurated—the so-called sexual revolution of the twentieth century.

Not that they always did so intentionally. One of the great Victorian sex scandals involved a prominent member of William Gladstone's cabinet, Sir Charles Dilke; his inability either to hush it up or fully to defend himself meant the ruin of a brilliant career. Gladstone's great Tory rival, Benjamin Disraeli, had predicted that Dilke would succeed the Whig prime minister. After 1885 that prospect was dead.

In that year, a young and pretty society wife, Virginia Crawford, told her husband Donald that she had been having an affair with their friend Charles Dilke. Her motive was unclear: it may have been that the affair was over and that she felt betrayed, or that she was jealous of other women in Dilke's life, or even that she had *not* had sexual relations with the eminently eligible cabinet member and was certain that other women had. She was a young woman of some charm; she was also nervous to the point of hysteria. True or not, the story she told to her husband was that Dilke had seduced her shortly after her marriage in 1882 (when she was eighteen and he, thirty-eight). She added that both her own maid and her own mother had been Dilke's mistresses. Donald Crawford sued for divorce, and the trial was held in 1886.

Dilke, a dynamic reformer, had been married in 1872; his wife died during childbirth in 1874. For the next ten years—as so much of the trial testimony asserted—the widower had one sexual experience after another. Perhaps the most striking thing about this testimony, at least if Virginia Crawford was in any way to be believed, concerned the easy compliance of all the maids, married women, and mothers involved. Even if Sir Charles was a man of unusually attractive person and personality, his successes would indicate that Victorian prudery among well-reared women and their women servants was more a conventional assumption than a fact.

Dilke denied the charge of adultery, and a number of eminent persons supported him. One, surprisingly, was Cardinal Manning, the highest-placed member of the Roman Catholic clergy in England. Another was the widow of Mark Pattison (a distinguished university don and biographer); she announced at the height of the scandal that she had become engaged to marry Dilke. He was surprised, but they *were* married, and apparently it was a happy union.

Dilke was compromised, but the judge dismissed the case against him and inconsistently granted Crawford a divorce. Divorce in Great Britain had been possible without a special act of Parliament since 1857; but it was still so rare, so strange, and so complicated, that the inconsistency and arbitrariness in this case were not especially surprising.

Still, Dilke's trials were not over. When a question was raised as to Virginia Crawford's sanity, the divorce case was reopened. At this point, Dilke found himself not only deserted by some former friends but, in one instance, betrayed. Or at least that was how it must have seemed to him. W. T. Stead, the radical Whig editor of the *Pall Mall Gazette,* had been a friend and supporter. He was himself experienced in adversity, if only briefly; in 1885, as part of a crusade against child prostitution, he bought a thirteen-year-old girl from her parents for five pounds and publicized the fact—only to be imprisoned for three months. Stead had, to begin with, been sympathetic toward Dilke. At the time of the second trial, he turned against his former friend and suggested in *Gazette* articles that Dilke was a libertine hardly better than those who bought and paid for underage and innocent prostitutes.

When the case was reopened, Sir Charles asked to be reinstated as a party to the suit, but his request was denied. Mrs. Crawford testified that she had had intercourse with Dilke and other men, and that he had indulged in sexual relations with a large number of women—including her mother. Citing her testimony, the prosecution charged the cabinet minister with "having committed adultery with the child of one friend and the wife of another." The divorce was confirmed. Dilke's political career was at an end.

Dilke's trials and fall were traumatic—for many earnest Victorians as well as for him. But revelations such as this about politicians and other public figures were not really so scandalous, or such clear instances of rebellion against the conventional moral code, as were what a series of artists and authors did and, above all, wrote about sex, love, and marriage.

We usually think that a Victorian attitude towards sex means not talking about sex and limiting, or pretending to limit, it to normal intercourse between husband and wife. The sanctity of marriage and the home! This is supposed to be the Victorian ideal. And it was an idea cherished by many, an idea given almost universal lip service. So it seems all the more surprising that among those who attacked the institution of marriage in this period—those who boldly rebelled against the strict stereotype of the strong husband and his dependent wife, held together by an unbreakable bond—were some of the prominent figures now thought of as being most staunchly and typically Victorian. They were not necessarily the ones who went furthest sexually, these public rebels. But they often had a great deal to lose.

Of course, like any other, the Victorian Age had its wild ones, its private rebels against sexual customs—those who went far beyond what they were willing to talk about or openly defend. There was Dante Gabriel Rossetti, for example, with his intense erotic drive and his long string of mistresses. And there was Rossetti's close friend Swinburne, who horrified so many Victorians with his poetic hints about strange and unsavory sexual doings—and who loved above all to be beaten, to be given masochistic pleasure which was explicitly sexual and which he could derive in no other way. About these and others, more later. To begin with, however, we might consider some eminent and vulnerable Victorians who undertook to make more or less direct attacks on both marriage and hypocritical morality: eminent Victorians who did so (partly, at least) for personal as well as for philosophical reasons.

John Stuart Mill, Robert Browning, and George Meredith— these are great names in the pantheon of English writers, and all these great Victorians raised radical questions about sexual freedom, challenging the belief that the only right kind of sex life was the standardized, "normal," immutable life of the married. In one way or another, each of these men was concerned personally about sexual orthodoxy, convention, and repression.

When he was a fairly young man at the height of his powers, Mill fell in love with a married woman, a woman who could not or would not get a divorce. At just about the same period in his life, Browning, too, fell in love—with an older woman. After some wooing and persuading, he eloped with her. For years afterward, he wrote poems about elopement, about marriage, both repressive and open, and even about free and adulterous love. Finally, George Meredith had sexual experiences both disillusioning and revealing. His first wife, who also was some years older than he, had an affair with another man, a painter. The result was a bastard child—and (once more!) an elopement.

But what these three eminent Victorian writers had in common was less their unorthodox lives and marriages— (as we have seen, there was plenty of unorthodox sexual activity going on) than their radical commentaries on sex, on the relations between the sexes, and in particular, on the nature of marriage. They were concerned with the right of women—and, not so incidentally, of men—to be sexually and legally independent persons rather than just mates. They were good Victorian Englishmen, but they were rebels against the traditional code of marriage— against what has, ironically, come to be thought of in our day as the "Victorian" code of sexuality.

2
Victorian
Rebels

The ex-parte marriage code, absurdly called the marriage contract, partakes no more of the nature of contracts than state
codes or any other codes of law made without the consent of
those whose happiness they affect.

(William Thompson, 1825)

Marriage in the abstract has always seemed to me the most profoundly indecent of ideas .... *Marriage* as it exists on all sides
of us, is ... an *abomination*.

(Elizabeth Barrett Browning, 1853)

What is any respectable girl brought up to do but to catch
some rich man's fancy and get the benefit of his money by marrying him?—as if a marriage ceremony could make any difference in the right or wrong of the thing!

(George Bernard Shaw, 1894)

17

There were not many middle- and upper-class Victorians, orthodox or not, who failed to take marriage very seriously indeed. For the ordinary, tax-paying, church-going, respectable married man, and thus for his wife as well, marriage represented the legitimizing of sex. But it also represented the basis of the family, which of course was in turn the basis of the state. So adultery—to say nothing of free love and direct assaults upon the marriage code—threatened an undermining not only of the family but also of the body politic. The identification of sexual license with social subversion is made explicit by Alfred Tennyson in his *Idylls,* where the adulterous love of bold Guinevere and bumbling Lancelot is blamed for the collapse of Arthur's realm, for the rending apart of the whole social fabric.

To other Victorians, marriage meant even more: it meant something profoundly grander—or profoundly worse!

There was the traditional Roman Catholic and Anglican view that marriage was a sacrament, blessed by the church as an expression of love and a proper channeling for human sexual urges—urges justified rationally by the need for procreation— but also as a symbolic representation of God's love. For many people over many generations, this doctrine had been simplified into the equation: omnipotent and infallible God equals man; weak and fallible creature equals woman. Of course, beginning in the fifth and sixth centuries, this equation was largely offset by the development of Mariolatry, the veneration of Mary that became almost worship: not only did Mary tend to replace feminine and human figures in those pagan religions from which Christianity was winning converts; but she also gave real women a virtually divine model and, especially in the later middle ages, provided a religious counterpart for the feminine ideal celebrated in chivalric codes and the love songs of the troubadors. In the nineteenth century, a potential conflict between religion and secular sex all seemed to be coming to a head. The Augustine-Calvin tradition tended to assume that sex was sin (in or out of marriage), and that was that. But the more orthodox development in religion glorified marriage and used sex as a divine allegory. The Biblical story of Adam and Eve, as usually interpreted, encouraged the primacy of man and the inferior role of wife and woman. But the medieval world to which so many Victorians looked back with longing had idealized women. Many mildly thoughtful but muddled Victorians compromised by believing (or trying to believe) that sex was sin outside of marriage and divine within it, that women were socially and intellectually inferior to men but—if they were married and faithful—they were theoretically and morally superior to the brutes.

In a century so worried about sexuality and so puzzled about the relation between sex and religion, the sacramental quality of married love became especially important. The Victorian writer most concerned with that relation—and easily the most sex-obsessed of English nineteenth-century poets—was Coventry Kersey Dighton Patmore.

For this odd, dogmatic, and remarkably sensual poet, true religion was "of all things the least sensual and the most sexual." The paradox was the paradox of Patmore's life. A good many eminent Victorians, including John Ruskin, Robert Browning,

and Dante Gabriel Rossetti, were his friends. (He was a contributor to Rossetti's pre-Raphaelite journal, *The Germ*.) But
the most important relationships in his life were with women
—with the pious, bright, and interesting poet Alice Meynell,
the Roman Catholic answer to Christina Rossetti, but also with
a series of more or less remarkable women whom he married.

He was married three times and outlived two of his wives.
He married the first, Emily Andrews, in 1847; she died in 1862.
At the time of his third marriage, to Harriet Robson, Patmore
was close to sixty.

But his second wife gave him the greatest inspiration, both
religious and sexual—as well as enough money to live on comfortably as a gentleman. Marianne Byles was a Roman Catholic
—they met in Rome, and after meeting her, the poet was
promptly converted from the Church of England to Catholicism.
She was also rich. Immediately following their marriage, Patmore
resigned his position as a minor assistant in the British Museum
(a job he got through the influence of that notorious libertine,
Monckton Milnes) and moved with his new wife to the country.
There he devoted himself to writing poems about the joys of
marriage, about sex and religious mysticism, or perhaps, about
sex as religious mysticism.

Patmore's major work up to this time was a long narrative in
verse, *The Angel in the House*, dedicated to Emily, his first wife.
This was a fairly bland story, a paean to wedded bliss in which
he first made clear his worshipful devotion to that angelic being,
the Wife, and his firm conviction that in matters intellectual,
social, and sexual, that mentally inferior angel must defer to her
Man. He also made clear—in the "Wedding Sermon" section of
the poem—that marriage ties must be legally as well as sacramentally firm. The argument is rather remarkable, coming from
a self-proclaimed wife-worshipper: if a man were able to divorce
his wife, Patmore's preacher tells us, he might be tempted to do
so whenever he saw a prettier or a more sexually attractive
woman. Perhaps more significantly, there is no suggestion that a
woman ever might want to break the marriage bond.

Patmore's later poetry went further yet in exalting marriage.
His series of odes called *The Unknown Eros* virtually made this

sexual sacrament the central one for Christianity, replacing the
Eucharist or Holy Communion. He went far enough, in fact, to
make some fellow Catholics like John Henry Newman and his
friend, Jesuit poet Gerard Manley Hopkins, nervous. No wonder.
Some of the implications in these odes seem rather odd, even
startling, when we find such things in supposedly religious verse.
Patmore glorified sexual intercourse in very nearly specific terms.
For example, in "Wind and Water," a poem about "wedding
light and heat," he compares sexual penetration to the action of
elemental forces:

> And all the heaving ocean heaves one way
> .   .   .   .   .
> Until the vanward billows feel
> The agitating shallows, and divine the goal.

He saw in the cross a phallic symbol. But the most extraordinary
idea in Patmore's later poems is his version of chastity. A modern
scholar (himself an Anglo-Catholic) points out, with candor and
with some dismay, that Patmore's purest mystical and "sacramental" experience amounted to *coitus interruptus*. This practice had been treated earlier in English poetry: by Rochester, for
instance, whose poems about getting drunk with a mistress and
having intercourse, but withdrawing before climax, may imply
an almost sadistic attitude—certainly not a worshipful one—
toward women. The subject had never before appeared in avow-
edly mystical poetry.

In some ways, unique as he seemed, Coventry Patmore might
be called a fairly typical Victorian—except that he carried certain Victorian attitudes to extremes. He was very conscious of sex
and often conscious of nothing else. Yet he could seem almost
antisexual. His poem "Lilian," about a "melancholy whore,"
demonstrated the effect of French novels on naive young readers.
Patmore's fevered descriptions of beautiful women's waists and
breasts combined oddly with a theoretical purity, if not puritanism—an attitude that made marriage a strict necessity.

Commenting on his own poem "Tamerton Church Yard,"
he said that marriage was "generally necessary to salvation."

Saint Paul and the early church fathers would have been startled by that bit of theology.

In praising marriage and wives, Patmore used language that was familiar in Victorian popular writing. The true wife, the good woman, was an "angel" or a "goddess" or a "pure spirit." (Patmore finally settled on an "angel.") This exaltation of women implies that the false wife or the imperfect woman is not angel but demon, not goddess but beast, not pure spirit but sullied and disgusting flesh.

Such extreme judgments upon women are common in the poems and pictures of the time. D. G. Rossetti's women are either ethereal maidens—usually blonde—or fallen and fatal creatures —usually brunette. He drew his blonde wife as an angel and his dark mistress as the adulterous Guinevere. As for Tennyson, in his *Idylls,* Merlin replies to the evil Vivien when she says tauntingly that men can never mount as high as women can, "we [men] scarce can sink as low": "men at most differ as Heaven and earth,/ But women, worst and best, as Heaven and Hell." The best also implies the worst. If a woman is supposed to be a deity or angel and displays some qualities that are less than divine or angelic, she becomes—in some men's eyes—either a hellcat or a lower beast. Women, from this point of view, belong either on a pedestal or in a sty; there is no in-between.

Psychologists call this attitude the madonna-harlot syndrome. It accounts for some criminal aberrations, such as that of Jack the Ripper, the Victorian terror who killed only whores or similarly loose women. (Incidentally, some modern historians argue that the mysterious Jack was of royal blood, was in fact one of Queen Victoria's sons.) This syndrome stems from a deep anxiety about sex that has led men, modern as well as Victorian, to project their own impulses upon the object of them.

It led Victorian journalists, moralists, and artists to translate that ancient myth, the Fall of Man, into a relatively modern version—or at least an updating of the medieval versions based on Eve as temptress—which might be called the Fall of Woman.

The Fallen Woman is, of course, commonplace in Victorian melodrama. She was found, too, in works of literature and art

that at least pretended to some seriousness. One example is a
three-part painting by a popular artist with the improbable name
of Augustus Egg. Called *Past and Present,* it uses elaborate ico-
nography and allegorical detail to tell the story of a faithless
wife, who is first shown prior to her banishment from home, husband, and children. A letter, presumably from her lover, is inter-
cepted by the pained and upright husband; later, this lover seems
to have abandoned her just as the husband has. In the last scene,
the adulterous wife is reduced to an almost animal existence,
huddling with her certainly illegitimate baby on a cold night beneath a bridge.

In no Victorian work of art or literature, however, is there a
sexually fallen man. Even Tennyson's Lancelot retains what the
poet must have thought of as a superior tone by talking priggishly of stainless virtue to the woman he has seduced—and with
whom he is still sleeping at the time of his pious sententiousness.

The notorious double standard implied here and, above all,
the extent to which marriage had become a yoke for women but
not necessarily for men, were being pointed out vigorously from
the late eighteenth century on. In 1792 Mary Wollstonecraft published her pioneering *Vindication of the Rights of Women.* In
1825 William Thompson brought out a tract with the succinct
title—very nineteenth century in style—*Appeal by One Half the
Human Race, Women, Against the Pretensions of the Other
Half, Men, to Retain Them in Political and Thence in Civil and
Domestic Slavery.* In 1835, the influential reformer Robert
Owen delivered his *Lectures on the Marriages of the Priesthood
of the Old Immoral World,* attacking religious institutions, private property, and above all, marriage as it then existed, marriage as either an *ex parte* code or a religious sacrament.

The widespread and fairly effective agitation for women's
rights was a Victorian movement, a movement that received its
greatest general attention in the second half of Victoria's reign.
(One talking point for the agitators was the anomaly that, in a
nation ruled by a woman, women had no political rights.) We
may think now of nineteenth-century feminism as being concerned primarily with the right to vote. And that *was* the issue
that gave focus to its energies late in the period. The suffragettes

of the 1890s and the early decades of the 1900s were in a tradition of seeking power through the ballot. This is itself a Victorian tradition. It was 1832, the year of the first great Reform Bill, that is generally thought of as the beginning of the era, rather than 1837, the date of Victoria's accession. Furthermore, the social-political history of Victorian and modern times is likely to emphasize the enlarging of the vote, up to the point of so-called universal suffrage. The stress in early Victorian feminism, however—in pamphlets and in public debate—was less on laws governing the voting franchise (after all, a vast number of men could not vote) than on laws governing marriage.

It can be argued that the attack on established marriage was something more radical than the later attack on discrimination at the polls. If that was so, the suffrage campaign represented a retreat. It can certainly be argued that John Stuart Mill's later work on the whole subject, his great essay *On the Subjection of Women,* involved more strategy than candor. It may have been a necessary strategy at a time when even women of genius—George Eliot above all, but also Elizabeth Barrett Browning, Elizabeth Gaskell, and a good many others—hardly dared speak out, so that the most vocal women's rights advocates were men! At any rate, the most widely effective of Victorian feminist works was Mill's book, a book that urged civil rights for women while (if cautiously and only by implication) it raised serious questions about the sacredness and justice of marriage laws.

On the Subjection of Women was published late in Mill's career, in 1869. But its prototype was an unpublished essay written by Mill much earlier, in 1832. In that essay, the attack on marriage and the arguments both for divorce and for free sexual choice were much more daring, more extreme, than those advanced in the book.

The real starting point for both essay and book, however, was a single event. The story of Mill's ardent interest—not just his opinion—as to questions of marriage and women's rights began at a dinner party given by a rich merchant and his wife in London during the summer of 1830.

John Stuart Mill was twenty-five, a young man with the look of an intellectual, with high forehead, soft curly hair, sharp fea-

tures—and a remarkably sharp mind in debate. According to a
contemporary:

> His manners were plain, neither graceful nor awkward; his
> features refined and regular; his eyes small relatively to
> the scale of the face, the jaw large, the nose straight and
> finely shaped, the lips thin and compressed, the forehead
> and head capacious; and both face and body seemed to
> represent outwardly the inflexibility of the inner man. He
> shook hands with you from the shoulder.

Young Mill had a promising career ahead of him: he was already becoming known as the rising star of the Philosophical
Radicals, the party that advocated franchise reform and free
trade, and he was already expected to be the first of the so-called
Utilitarians to succeed in politics. Who could say how brilliant
that career might be? Literary triumphs (he was a frequent contributor to the Utilitarian *Westminster Review*), Parliament,
and perhaps at last the prime minister's office! After all, he had
a first-rate mind, a lucid style in writing and speaking, the support of powerful friends, youth, and energy. All that he lacked
was love.

That, at least, is one way of interpreting the "crisis in [his]
mental history" that Mill had gone through almost four years
earlier, a time of nervous depression that he described in his
autobiography much later. He had been brought up by his
father, James Mill, and by the rationalist philosopher Jeremy
Bentham to be a thinking machine—without affection, without
passion, without humor. (Bentham's lack of humor may be suggested by his willing his body to the University of London for
embalming and display; the body remained in a university build-
ing for years, enclosed within a glass case, the mummified head
perched between the feet.) His mother had been remote, his
father cold and demanding. At the age of four, he could read
Greek; at the age of twenty, he had never loved or been loved by
anyone.

Mill had tried to rally from a nervous breakdown by reading
poetry, by cultivating his feelings through books. But in 1830 he
vaguely felt the need of something else. He was past adolescence.
He was becoming financially independent, or reasonably so. Now

the appropriate thing to do, the rational thing, was to look for a wife. He admitted to his friend John Sterling that he was lonely. But he put the matter in a characteristically dry and rational way: he lacked a "fellow traveller," a human being "who acknowledges a common object with me, or with whom I can cooperate." This is not the language of passionate yearning. Yet, ironically, passion did break into the young Mill's life—at the wrong time and in the wrong way, from any conventionally moral or wholly rational point of view—at that dinner party that summer evening.

It must have been a remarkable evening—more remarkable, of course, than anyone present could then have known. Mill went with his two closest friends, John Roebuck—the energetic India-born young man who was to become Matthew Arnold's butt thirty-five years later because of his smugness about the state of England—and George Graham—like Mill, a promising young writer for the *Westminster*. Harriet Martineau was there too, the stern feminist writer who had surmounted amazing difficulties: she was alone in the world, she had been poverty-stricken, and she was ugly and stone-deaf. This dinner, then, was a gathering of serious young radicals and intellectuals, Utilitarians and Unitarians, rationalists and "friends of the species." But into that unlikely setting "a passion sprang out of the bushes like a hundred Ashantees, and [Mill] was carried away captive."

There was another important person present that evening, in fact, the person who brought John Mill to meet the host and hostess—but especially to meet the hostess. It is not at all clear if this person, the eminent Unitarian clergyman William Johnson Fox, intended that sexual passion should spring out of the bushes at Mill and at the hostess, too. But it does seem clear that he was arranging for the lonely bachelor and the lonely wife to meet.

The lonely wife was Harriet Taylor, twenty-three years old and eleven years younger than her husband John. Both her husband and she were members of Fox's congregation at the South Place Chapel. Although she had been a devoted wife and mother for the four years of her marriage, she had only recently told the magnetic Fox that she felt some lack in her domestic life, a lack of intellectual stimulation and perhaps of excitement. For all his estimable qualities, her older husband—a conscientious man, a prominent Unitarian layman, a sympathizer with political reform, as well as a successful businessman—was not a satisfactory intellectual companion. At least, he was not very lively. So she told Fox.

And lively, Harriet Taylor *was*. Lively, imaginative, and beautiful. In spite of her actual stature—she was not much more than five feet—she struck people as being tall and willowy, like a true Victorian heroine. In fact, crusty Thomas Carlyle, who later grew to dislike the woman, described her about this time as "a living romance heroine, of the clearest insight, of the royalest volition, very interesting, of questionable destiny."

The violent Carlyle, already on his way to being the arch-reactionary of the age, might have put the last point much more strongly if he had guessed that his "romance heroine" was to be the great inspiration for the most effective mid-Victorian attacks upon male supremacy and the old sexual order. When Jane Carlyle once spoke in defense of a woman who had eloped with a lover, her husband cursed her as the "advocate of whores"; his policy, private as well as public, was that " 'the man should bear rule in the house, and not the woman'—this is an eternal axiom, the law of nature, which no mortal departs from unpunished." Carlyle, like Ruskin after him, was fond of expressing his prejudices as eternal axioms and laws of nature.

Later, Thomas Carlyle grew so suspicious of Harriet Taylor that he blamed her for one of the great temporary shocks to his literary career. One gloomy evening in March, 1835, John Mill burst in upon the Carlyles, staggering, his face ashen. He asked Jane Carlyle to go downstairs to the carriage where Mrs. Taylor was waiting. Both she and her astonished husband at once assumed that the two were at last running off together to live in adultery; but, as he must have been preparing a thunderous denunciation, Carlyle learned the truth. The handwritten and only existing copy of Carlyle's work about the French Revolution, the work to which he had devoted several years and which Mill had borrowed—had been destroyed! The explanation was that an ignorant housemaid had used the sheets of paper to start a fire.

From much later evidence, that seems to have been the truth. But Carlyle always believed that Mill had given the manuscript to Harriet Taylor, who had either lost or destroyed it.

What was this person of such "questionable destiny" really like? An 1834 portrait of her shows a simply-dressed young woman with light brown curls, enormous dark eyes set off by a pale complexion, and all in all, an air of thoughtfulness.

She was beautiful, young, intelligent, extremely sensitive and —of questionable destiny! It must have dawned slowly upon the thoughtful young Harriet that her destiny might not be simply that of a devoted wife and loving mother of two—soon to be three—children. The man who was so struck by her at dinner soon became a regular visitor to the Taylor house on Christopher Street. Possibly some gleam in his eye, some fervency in his manner, had indicated almost at once Mill's more than casual and certainly more than intellectual interest. In any event, however careful Mill may or may not have been, it seems unlikely that Harriet Taylor was shocked by any suggestion that would lead to stretching or even breaking the marriage bond. Under the influence of Fox and of Harriet Martineau, she had been writing papers and letters on the role of women and on marriage. And, unlike Harriet Martineau, she knew as a wife what she was writing about:

> Marriage is the only contract ever heard of, of which a necessary condition in the contracting parties was, that one should be entirely ignorant of the nature and terms of the contract. For owing to the voting of chastity as the greatest virtue of women, the fact that a woman knew what she undertook would be considered just reason for preventing her undertaking it.

In a letter she wrote:

> Women are educated for one single object, to gain their living by marrying (some poor souls get it without church going in the same way—they do not seem to me a bit worse than their honoured sisters) —to be married is the object of their existence and that being gained they do really cease to exist as to anything worth calling life or any useful pur-

pose. . . . I have no doubt that when the whole community
is really educated, though the present laws of marriage were
to continue they would be perfectly disregarded, because no
one would marry.

In an unpublished paper on the "Education of Women," she
commented:

All that has yet been said respecting the social condition of
women goes on the assumption of their inferiority. People
do not complain of their state being degraded at all—they
complain only that it is *too much* degraded.

This does not sound much like a romance heroine, let alone a
conventional Victorian wife and mother.

It was this unconventional strong-mindedness that, along
with Harriet's charming manner and beauty, attracted Mill.
Slightly later, he wrote in a letter:

The women I have known, who possessed the highest mea-
sure of what are considered feminine qualities, have combined with them more of the highest *masculine* qualities
than I have ever seen in but one or two men, and those
one or two men were also in many respects almost women.
I suspect it is the second-rate people of the two sexes that
are unlike. The first rate are alike in both—except—no, I
do not think I can except anything—but then, in this respect, my position has been and is, what . . . every human
being's is in many respects, "a peculiar one."

Soon, Mill's familiarity with the Taylors was quite clearly a
matter of his interest in Harriet—and of her interest in him.
They talked at length, they corresponded, she took his advice
about her writing, and she strengthened him in his own ideas—
including his opposition to the elder Mill's view that women
were adequately protected by the enfranchisement and legal
rights of fathers and husbands. (William Thompson's 1825
broadside had been a direct attack on James Mill's position.) On
that and related matters, she transformed Mill's first mild and
theoretical beliefs into passionate convictions. By early 1832, he
was fully aware that marriage and divorce were not, for him, issues in the abstract; he was deeply in love with a married woman.

Harriet was just as aware of the situation. She agreed with—

and brought Mill around as well to agreeing with—the opinions of Robert Owen: "*Chastity,* sexual intercourse *with* affection. *Prostitution,* sexual intercourse *without* affection"; "the indissolubility of marriage is the keystone of woman's present lot... and must be reconstructed"! But by now she was the mother of three children. Divorces in Victorian England were still rare and difficult to obtain; and after a divorce, the father—even if he were an adulterer, a sadist, a wife-beater, a drunkard—always got custody of the children. There simply could not be a divorced woman bringing up her own child.

John Taylor was no adulterer, much less any of those other things. When, in 1832, his wife told him that she loved Mill, he was distressed, pained, and deeply perplexed. He asked her, for the sake of her home and children, to give up seeing Mill, at least for now. That temporary and uneasy state of affairs could not have continued long; but he was too fair and kind to disown her —and too inept to find a better solution.

The matter may have been complicated by a parallel development. Harriet's mentor, William Johnson Fox, who had introduced her to Mill, was neither very young nor physically striking, with his moon face and portly build; but he was magnetic, eloquent, vivid—and married to a particularly dull wife. He also had two beautiful wards, Sarah and Eliza Flower; and he was in love with one of them.

The Flower sisters were remarkable for their beauty but remarkable in other ways as well. Sarah wrote songs and hymns (including "Nearer, My God, to Thee"), went on the stage, produced a book-length poem about the early Christian martyrs, and died young of consumption. The younger Eliza, or Lizzie, was more subject and inspirer of art than creator; Robert Browning, who fell in love with her when an adolescent, represented her as *Pauline* in his first published book of poetry. Lizzie Flower was Harriet Taylor's best friend. And she became the mistress of her guardian, Fox.

It was a scandal and a problem. It was a problem especially for poor Mrs. Fox, trying to keep her children and her household in order while it became more and more apparent to the servants, to the neighbors, to the members of her husband's congregation, that the pale and fragile young woman who was supposedly the minister's ward—she was aptly named Flower!—was actually living in sin with him. The wife retired to the upper part of the house. She wrote to her husband asking for a separation and for support. (He could not afford it, he replied.) She complained, at last, to friends, to the solid laymen at the South Place Chapel. And the fat was in the fire.

When the scandal broke, the richest and most respected Unitarian congregation in London was almost split apart. Fox, who had already expressed advanced views on the relations between the sexes in his journal *The Monthly Repository,* believed that his adulterous relationship with his ward was no business of the chapel members—if, indeed, it was adulterous—and at this point he neither admitted nor denied the charge.

Harriet Taylor and John Mill rallied to the minister's support. Mill thought privately, perhaps naïvely, that Fox had not had sexual relations with Lizzie. What Harriet thought, or possibly knew, we cannot be sure. The extraordinary fact is that the Fox faction won—that in 1834 it was possible for a prominent dissenting clergyman to be accused, and virtually convicted, of adultery and to retain his pulpit. After his victory Fox moved out of the old home and set up housekeeping with Lizzie in Bayswater; now there was no doubt as to the situation. The minister's wife and children had a settlement, and he was openly living with the woman he loved.

Even now, even when other radicals and feminists like Harriet Martineau violently disapproved, Harriet Taylor and John Mill remained loyal to Fox and Lizzie. Yet they could not follow their example, as Fox firmly advised them to do.

Mill's biographer has said of him and Harriet at this point, "she was neither his mistress in one sense, nor was she less than that in another." Still, Harriet Taylor had an attentive and suffering husband as well as an attentive and suffering lover. And both of them, perhaps *all* of them, were frustrated in this tense triangle of highminded, rational people—people more passionate, it may well be, than they admitted or wanted to be. The husband sent his wife to a house in Kent. There she was visited almost every weekend by her lover, with her baby daughter Helen acting as chaperone. But her husband and other children visited her there, too. It was, to say the least, an odd arrangement.

The arrangement was never to be comfortable. Mill wanted, understandably, to present the woman he loved to the society of his friends and acquaintances. He took her to an evening party given by the Charles Bullers, and the result was a minor social shock. There was no clear, direct snub, but the point was made clear to both of them that London society was not altogether ready to receive a married woman in the company of a single man who was generally supposed to be her lover. Even hearty, friendly Roebuck, virtually Mill's best friend, went to see him the next day at his office in India House to warn him how disastrous this public affair could be for his career. Mill heard Roebuck out and coolly said good-bye. At that point, as Roebuck soon realized, their friendship ended.

However, Mill was aware how dangerous for his beloved the whole thing was. He reminded her what social disaster could attend the daring women who eloped with lovers. He may have been reminding himself what blight the life of a promising young man in politics and public life might suffer. At any rate, he did nothing—and she did nothing.

And so the painful triangle—painful for husband, wife, and lover—remained just that.

Except for Fox, Mill's friends and family were less than sympathetic. Old James Mill disapproved violently of his son's being in love with another man's wife. Thomas Carlyle, who had hoped John Stuart Mill would be his disciple, withheld comment for a time, but there was no possible doubt as to his attitude: he believed in the absolute force of the marriage vow and in the absolute power of the husband over the wife.

No doubt even the stolen moments of these two lovers involved problems and anxieties. In 1836 John Mill was in a state of near collapse. Some critics have said that he was suffering from sexual starvation, from overexcitement and frustration, but the fact that his father died that year may also have had something to do with it. He took a leave from his office and editorial duties, meeting Harriet in Paris. But neither of them was alone. Mill had his two younger brothers with him. Harriet had her three children and a nurse. They went on to Switzerland as a party, and the lovers were glad to be together; but clearly it was not an elopement or an escape from duty or even a wholly carefree holiday. The families still impinged; the lovers were still, both of them, caught up in their frustrating situation.

In the following years, Mill was distracted by his work as editor of the (renamed) *London and Westminster Review* and by his political activity. All the time he remained a friend of the Taylor household, even though he and the husband of his beloved were no more than coolly polite; Mill and Taylor were associated in politics and as fellow founding members of the Reform Club. But John and Harriet were together, and away from others, as much as possible—taking walks in Regent's Park, discussing all his plans, and writing letters. She was his "Beauty," he was her "Caro." If there was nothing illicit about their relations in quite the usual meaning, there was certainly an air of intrigue and even, sometimes, of secrecy.

At Christmastime in 1838, John Taylor and his wife (while he lived she never ceased to regard herself as his wife) traveled with their daughter Helen, still hardly more than a baby, to Paris. There Harriet's husband left her and the child, returning to London. Mill arrived immediately; and wife, child, and lover proceeded to Italy, ultimately to Naples. From then until early spring John Mill and Harriet Taylor lived together in one part of Italy or another.

They lived together—but in what sense? Mill later declared they had been chaste at this period. That declaration might have been a piece of strategy in an argument for the rights of both men and women to private sexual decisions; since Mill also declared that they—and any other similarly situated couples—had a moral right to have private physical relations and that their doing so was no other person's concern. (Matthew Arnold, for one, was shocked: he thought it was just as disgusting to *advocate* adultery as to commit it.) The answer, then, to the question "in what sense?" is that we have no answer. Certainly, the relationship was in *some* sense sexual, involving physical as well as intellectual and temperamental attraction between a man and a woman. And it seems hard now to believe that the passionate language of Mill's and Harriet Taylor's letters did not ever find more direct expression. If the expression went no further than touches, kisses, perhaps caresses, the strain upon these two trapped young people must have been at times nearly unbearable. The strain lasted more than eighteen years! No wonder they both suffered a series of mysterious illnesses: John Mill's chest pains, disordered stomach, recurrent depressions; Harriet Taylor's periodic faintness and, beginning in 1841, a paralysis that temporarily cost her the use of her legs.

By 1848, when Mill published his *Political Economy*—his masterpiece, as most Victorians thought it—the Mill-Taylor triangle was familiar to everyone in London political and literary circles. Even so, Harriet's husband was sensitive enough about the awkwardness of his position to object when Mill proposed this dedication for his latest book:

TO
MRS. JOHN TAYLOR
As The Most Eminently Qualified
Of All Persons Known To The Author
Either To Originate Or To Appreciate
Speculations On Social Improvement,
This Attempt To Explain And Diffuse Ideas
Many Of Which Were First Learned From Herself,
Is
With The Highest Respect And Regard
Dedicated.

This extraordinary wording was printed in only a few gift copies.

Gossip, frustration, the strain of secret meetings—all of it continued to tell on the two lovers: in the 1840s, they virtually retired from society and gave up all their old friends except Fox (himself alone since the death of his Lizzie). But, after all, the husband's lot was probably the worst of all. Harriet, if gossiped about, was at least an interesting figure; she had the good sense to be loved by two eminent men, one rich and one a genius. Mill had his political activity, his writing, his editing—and Harriet's devotion. John Taylor was respected but unloved, wealthy but

not particularly well; his consolations were good food and wine.
For more than eighteen years he obliged his wife and Mill with
his tolerance, his long-suffering kindness. Finally, in 1849, he did
the most obliging thing of all: he died.

On Easter Monday, 1851, after long months of public
mourning and private debate about the future, Harriet Hardy
Taylor and John Stuart Mill were married. Would their marriage now seem to justify the lewder gossip of the past? Would
Mill be accused of wanting the money left by the man he had,
supposedly, already wronged?

Together at last, they were more than ever an isolated
couple—except for Harriet's loyal children, especially Helen.
They had cut themselves off from friends and families, both
Hardys and Mills. Neither was in good health. Harriet con-
tracted her husband's severe consumption, from which he was to
recover but which was to kill her. Yet their married life together
was essentially happy. They traveled to the seashore, to Scotland,
to the continent. They discussed Mill's projects, including the
great essay *On Liberty,* later to be dedicated to Harriet as con-
taining ideas that were mostly hers. They conferred over daughter
Helen's career as an actress. The marriage lasted less than seven
years. This was almost certainly the happiest time of Mill's life.

Harriet Hardy Taylor Mill died in 1858.

Some ten years after her death, Mill published his book *On
the Subjection of Women.* It had been written soon after his
wife's death, in 1861; and it represents, along with the essay *On
Liberty,* the major intellectual result of their relationship.

The book was less daring than that essay of 1832, which had
been written specifically for Harriet Taylor (but not published
until 1951 because the public was not yet ready, or so Mill apparently believed, to be enlightened on the subject).

On the matter of divorce, for instance, a subject undoubtedly close to Mill's heart, the earlier essay revealed just what he
felt. The fact that marriage was so rigid a contract—that divorce
was so difficult—was "the keystone of woman's present lot."
(Like Meredith, Mill saw that this lot was something less than
idyllic.) The phrase jibes with the thoughts expressed in several
of Mill's letters. For example:

> My opinion on Divorce is that, though any relaxation of
> the irrevocability of marriage would be an improvement,
> nothing ought to be ultimately rested in short of entire free-
> dom on both sides to dissolve this like any other partnership.

Compare this statement with Harriet Taylor's peppery comment
of some forty years earlier: in an educated community, she declared, "the present laws of marriage would be perfectly disregarded, because no one would marry."

Now, contrast all these passages with the one on divorce in
The Subjection of Women, in which Mill subordinated the issue
to the more immediate one—so he thought—of woman's suffrage. In fact, he evaded the subject of divorce with what became
his standard political reaction to the question, saying that such
matters should not be decided "until women have an equal voice
in determining them, nor until there has been experience of the
marriage relation as it would exist between equals." Of course,
Mill was genuinely interested in the cause of women's suffrage
(the great Victorian radical assumption, from the 1830s on, was
that the ballot would go far to solve all social injustice); and he
came surprisingly close to achieving a majority vote in Parliament on this (not burning, but smoldering) issue—an issue that
had also been of some concern to Harriet Taylor, who had published in 1851 an essay on the "Enfranchisement of Women."

But if his "official formula" on divorce, as St. John Packe
calls it, was both earnest and politic, it now seems inadequate.
Mill seems to have forgotten that the longed-for equality of
women with men could hardly be achieved *until* the tyranny of
Victorian marriage laws had been broken: the franchise was not,
and could not be, in itself the single or final step in freeing
women, a kind of liberation from which all others would auto-
matically flow. Mill also seems to have forgotten—again, perhaps, because he was an active political strategist—the passionate
conviction that the young bachelor in love once displayed on precisely these vexed subjects of marriage and divorce.

Yet, whatever the modification—whether expansion, toning
down, or pointing up—the spirit of the book was the spirit of the
essay. It may not be exaggeration to say that it was the spirit of
Harriet Hardy Taylor Mill.

Mill did insist in his autobiography that, although she altered his thinking in other areas, Harriet Taylor was not the source of his ideas in *The Subjection of Women*. In fact, he asserted that his conviction about the rights of women—what women *ought* to have—was precisely what interested her in him. But he admitted that his conviction was "in my mind, little more than an abstract principle."

And this is just the point: Harriet Hardy Taylor turned his abstract principle into fervent conviction—conviction that issued in writing, in speaking out publicly, and in political agitation. In this sense, Mill's meeting her was the beginning of his deep personal concern about the subjection of women—concern not only about theories but also about the reality. After all, for twenty years Harriet Taylor had been subjected to the kindest and most tolerant of husbands—but also to laws and conventions that denied her her freedom or that equated her freedom with social ruin, the loss of her children, and the destruction of her lover's career. Her subjection had been, at least psychologically, John Stuart Mill's own subjection.

The young Mill's behavior proved that serious, introspective, middle-class Victorian dissenters—the supposedly self-righteous Protestants, the very group that is blamed for, or credited with, the smugness and prudishness of English society in this era—could produce in life and literature a critical reaction to such conventionality. It proved further that these dissenters could produce impulses toward radical and effective reform concerning the sensitive subject of sex.

William Johnson Fox, Eliza Flower, Harriet Taylor and her suffragette daughter, Helen, and of course Mill himself—all were products of middle-class, mercantile, Protestant-Victorian England. So was Robert Browning.

Browning's tendency to be a rebel, perhaps more than Mill's, can be explained by heredity. For one thing, his ancestry was partly black. Unlike Alexandre Dumas (the elder), he made little of the fact. But his father may have been more conscious of it. Sent by the poet's grandfather to the West Indies, to his mother's sugar plantation, Browning's father was said to have

conceived such a hatred of the slave system . . . that he re-
linquished every prospect—supported himself, while there,
in some other capacity, and came back, while yet a boy, to
his father's profound astonishment and rage—one proof of
which was, that when he heard that his son was a suitor . . .
he benevolently waited on her uncle to assure him that his
niece would be thrown away on a man so evidently born
to be hanged!—those were his words.

This is the poet's own account, in a letter written to Elizabeth
Barrett before they were married. It shows both his admiration
for his father and his sense of how unjust his grandfather had
been. In other words, his feelings were both filial and rebellious.
And the combination of loyalty (to family, country, religion,
conventional and traditional values) with rebelliousness (against
familial tyranny, national insularity, bigotry, the repressiveness
of convention) suggests a duality that one finds throughout
Browning's work and life.

For example, in some true sense he certainly loved his wife,
who was a pious and strong-minded woman; but he gave every
literary evidence of a sense that marriage was a kind of prison
and that wives could be an awful bore. But of all that, more
later.

Going on about his father, the young poet—in the letter to
his wife-to-be—said that the elder Browning, who loved art, had
to "consume his life after a fashion he always detested." What he
detested was working as a senior clerk in the dreary Bank of
England.

Young Robert Browning was not brought up to be a bank
clerk; his father, unlike his father's father, had no intention of
imposing a life in commerce upon his boy. Perhaps, as Betty Miller suggests in her biography, the poet's mother was more strong-
willed about imposing *her* ideas and practice. In any event, Mrs.
Browning, the daughter of a Dundee shipowner and a conventionally pious woman of the Congregationalist persuasion
(though *persuasion* is perhaps not quite the right word since a
Congregationalist could be a Calvinist, a Unitarian, or just about
anything else), saw to it that her son came round—in spite of

Shelley and his youthful radicalism—to a semblance of proper
Christianity. This is, in part, the theme of Robert Browning's
first published poem, *Pauline*.

Of course, *Pauline* also was in part about Eliza Flower,
whom the adolescent Browning met—through his family's
"chapel" connections—when she was most delicate and beautiful. But the figure of the beautiful and beloved one appears only
briefly and vaguely at the beginning and end of the poem. For
the most part, this is a young man's tediously discursive look into
himself. When the poem appeared, Eliza showed it to her guardian, W. J. Fox, who by this time was probably also her lover. He
gave it a favorable review in his *Monthly Repository*. Fox also
gave the poem to Mill, for him to review; and Mill wrote two
notices of it, one for the *Examiner* and one for the *Edinburgh
Magazine*. As it happened, neither notice was published. But
Mill returned the poem to Fox with his notes; and, even though
he asked that these notes not be shown to the poet, Browning did
see them. Mill's comments began,

> With considerable poetic powers, the writer seems to me
> possessed with a more intense and morbid self-consciousness
> than I ever knew in any sane human being.

The burden of Mill's criticism was that this poem hardly concerned "Pauline" at all, that she was hardly a real person, that
the young man who was evidently both speaker and poet was
wrapped up in self-seeking, self-worshipping, and self-despising.
Mill wrote his remarks only a few years after he had met his Harriet, who inspired the passion that took him out of his own self-
analytical moods, his depressions. And of the younger (only six
years younger) Browning he wrote. "I know not what to wish for
him but that he may meet with a *real* Pauline."

Harriet's best friend, Eliza, was certainly not to be Browning's "*real* Pauline"; but Elizabeth Barrett was. It may even be
that Robert Browning's search for someone delicate and poetic to
love is what led him to this older woman (she was in fact just
Mill's age). He always enjoyed impressing older women; he impressed Eliza's hymn-writing sister Sarah so much with his Vol-

tairean arguments—when he was fifteen—that she told Fox her faith was in danger of being shaken. What he may have wanted unconsciously was a woman capable of impressing him.

In the fall of 1844 Robert Browning was thirty-two. He had published, besides the forgotten *Pauline,* his play *Paracelsus,* which was something of a critical success; the confused book-length poem *Sordello,* which was a puzzlement (Carlyle's wife Jane declared she had read it through without knowing if Sordello was a man, a city, or a book); and most of *Bells and Pomegranates,* including his first major poem, *Pippa Passes.* He was beginning to be known. Yet he was flattered and delighted to find his name mentioned in a volume of poems by one Elizabeth Barrett, along with the names of William Wordsworth and Alfred Tennyson. He wrote to her at once, beginning his letter, "I love your verses with all my heart."

She was thirty-nine and something of an invalid; the 1844 volume was her first significant original publication. But for some time she was to be better known than Browning as a poet. And the correspondence that immediately followed his first letter made it clear that she was indeed a woman capable of impressing him: William Clyde DeVane comments "that here at last, as John Stuart Mill had wished years ago, Browning attained complete convalescence."

Robert's wooing of Elizabeth has been the subject of scores of biographies, studies, plays, and even a movie or two. It is all too well-known to go over again in detail: the exchange of love letters for well over a year before he was allowed to see her; his ardent wooing; her father's adamant opposition; their elopement and escape to Italy. But the more romantic accounts of this affair have not always stressed how much daring they both displayed and how close they came to rebelling—more openly than Mill and Harriet Taylor—against the morality of their comfortable middle-class, Protestant, very proper world.

Elizabeth Barrett was **not a married woman**—although critics have had a Freudian heyday with her father's possessiveness, his jealousy, his (no doubt) sexually inspired and morbid attachment to his daughters. Yet she found the break with her family so painful a prospect that she took almost two years to decide in Browning's favor. Significantly, when she did decide, she was willing to go all the way.

Robert and Elizabeth met secretly during most of this period, when her father was away from the house on Wimpole Street. And what her wooer proposed, an elopement, an escape from Wimpole Street, involved yet more subterfuge—what for families like the Brownings and the Barretts was, to say the least, very unconventional behavior. From several reports it seems clear that Elizabeth, once she was persuaded to such a break with convention, would have been willing to dispense with the conventional gesture of a wedding before leaving England. In any event, in some later letters her comments about marriage as an institution (she called it "indecent," "an abomination") suggest that the lack of a license, ring, and ceremony would have been for her —privately at least—no great lack.

Robert Browning was always less daring in life than in poetry. They were secretly married in Marylebone Parish Church on September 9, 1846. On the 19th, they escaped together to the continent.

Over and over again in his later poetry, Browning told versions of this story, this one great act of daring in his life. A number of these versions actually encouraged the breaking of conventional rules about sexual behavior and marriage that Elizabeth and he had only bent. One might say that they advocated living in sin.

But almost as remarkable is the fact that some of the poems Browning wrote *before* his and Elizabeth Barrett's elopement anticipated that event. This young poet's fantasy about the daring rescue of a cloistered woman was spelled out in verse before it was acted out. In this way, as in other ways, Browning may have been imitating his early idol, Percy Bysshe Shelley.

"Mad Shelley," atheist and political radical, died when Browning was ten years old. But his spirit seemed to live on in the enthusiasms of the younger poet. Although Shelley was opposed to the marriage contract, he eloped with Harriet Westbrook. He married her when she was sixteen and he nineteen, in order to save the girl from her oppressive family. (He was not, he thought, in love with her; and the understanding was that each was free to form other connections.) A year or so later, he met Mary Wollstonecraft Godwin, daughter of two major figures in English radicalism, the arch-feminist Mary Wollstonecraft and the author of *Political Justice,* William Godwin. He was soon living with her; she bore him several children. Depressed, his wife Harriet committed suicide only five years after their marriage. Shelley became a scandalous figure. Victorians in general—but *not* Browning—were horrified by his sex life; and the scandal was intensified when he "rescued" young Emilia Viviani from a convent where, he said, she was a prisoner. (He also wrote a poem to her, "Epipsychidion," which was almost certainly platonic in the popular as well as the philosophical sense, but which most nineteenth-century readers took to be a declaration of adulterous passion.) The idea of saving an imprisoned woman is recurrent in Shelley's poetry. It is even more strikingly recurrent— in fact, almost obsessively so—in Browning's poetry.

Sometimes the prisoner did *not* elope. Browning's best-known poem, "My Last Duchess," is about a woman who was no more than a possession to her man, a woman who died having failed to escape from her connubial prison—just as "Count Gismond" is about the woman who did escape. The husband who speaks in the first poem is a prototype of the possessive husband in Browning's later verse and at the same time a shadowy version of Elizabeth Barrett's possessive father; the Count in the second poem represents Browning's familiar type of the daring lover— and his behavior predicts how Browning was to act.

Not only did life imitate art. It almost seems that Browning was looking for a way to fulfill his imagination—that he was looking for a woman who had to be rescued in a bold and unconventional way.

Still, Elizabeth Barrett was not really like the women in Shelley's life—at least, not like Harriet and Emilia. And she resembled Mary, the great feminist's daughter and author of *Frankenstein,* only in being a writer. Elizabeth was a dominating woman, as strong in her opinions and her forthright expression of them as Robert Browning's mother had been.

She took his mother's place and very largely ran his life, to the point of insisting that their son Pen wear his hair in long golden ringlets—rather like her own—long after he was an infant. When she died, the widower had his son's hair cut. Until then, this was apparently the way Robert Browning wanted things to be.

His life and art suggest that Robert Browning had two fantasies about his sexual life: that of the weak woman who must be saved from bondage and that of the strong woman who is to be revered and deferred to, as a mother.

Browning's attitudes toward sex and marriage were more complex than even these two fantasies might indicate. From the evidence of his poetry and letters, early and late, he was an intensely sexual man—and an extremely complicated one.

Part of the reason was that this man, who was first of all an artist, and who had ambitions to do painting, sculpture, and music as well as poetry, had always associated art with sex. From his writing, it seemed that making beautiful things and making love were closely related, if not virtually the same; and the important thing in both was the *process* rather than the poem, picture, statue, or symphony (or, for that matter, the baby—that was the end product).

So sex and art were, in Browning's imagination, forms of creativity that could be closely linked. He tended in poem after poem to make the true artist the ardent lover and to make the selfishly possessive husband—or guardian, or father-figure—a collector of art. But there was something problematic in his notion of the artist-lover, like Jules in *Pippa Passes* who vows to turn his simple, illiterate bride into his own ideal. And not until some time after his marriage did he begin faintly to perceive that there might be a parallel between the two ideas, that the idealizing lover who wants to create the ultimate being of his beloved is using her as raw material rather than accepting her as an individual—just as the collector-husband sees his wife as a possession, a mere thing.

Yet, for all his fancies and theories there is reason to believe that, at least before his marriage, he was fairly naïve about sex—about the facts and terms as well as the psychology of sexual relations. One of the most startling moments in his first successful poem, *Pippa Passes,* occurs when the innocent young title character sings her final song, comparing animals to people: "owls and bats,/ Cowls and twats,/ Monks and nuns!" Nobody has ever explained just what he thought he was writing.

The poems Browning wrote during his married years include a surprising number about serious problems in, or actual failures of, marriage.

There are, as well, expressions both direct and indirect of marital bliss, of ecstatic moments that were clearly moments of sexual rapture. This is true especially in *Men and Women,* a volume of poems that, as the title indicates, is mostly about the relations between the sexes. "Love is best!" the first of these poems declares. Another describes the sexual love of "our two souls/ [that] mix as mists do; each is sucked/ Into each now." This passage goes as far as Patmore ever did in evoking intercourse and climax: "a bar was broken between/ Life and life: we were mixed at last." One authority says that "the event which Browning describes ... had taken place at 50 Wimpole Street in London in 1845"—that is, before Robert and Elizabeth were married. If that is so, and if Browning the poet remembered .accurately, one can only comment that Browning the lover must have been remarkably ardent. Certainly Browning the husband appeared to be devoted. His wife is called "My Star," "Beatrice," "moon of poets," and finally (once more in the language of Patmore referring to *his* wife), "angel."

All of this sounds appropriate and suggests a happy aftermath to his ardent wooing, their love letters, and the romantic elopement. The curious fact, however, is that in the less personal, apparently dramatic, poems of this period, there is more about unhappiness in marriage than there is about wedded bliss. Although "A Lover's Quarrel" is presented as a dramatic work, the subjects over which Browning's lovers quarrel are the two main topics upon which Elizabeth and Robert Browning disagreed: spiritualism and Napoleon III. During the years they lived in Florence, she was a firm believer in the occult and at times thought herself to be a medium. She interested others, including the wife of Nathaniel Hawthorne, with whom she arranged seances, in psychic phenomena—to the disgust of both Hawthorne and Browning. To put it mildly, Browning was skeptical. Worse, he soon grew bored with the whole subject. (His opinion about the characters of professional spiritualists was expressed in "Mr. Sludge, 'The Medium' "—but that was not to be published until after his wife's death.) As for the Emperor of France, Elizabeth Browning admired him greatly while her husband was, again, a scoffer.

It seems remarkable how often Browning imagined, in the verse he wrote during his marriage, the experiences of love frustrated, love dying, love dead—usually within a marriage. The subject of the inconstant husband and the constant wife fascinated Browning. His fullest treatment of it was "James Lee's Wife," published (and probably written) after Elizabeth Browning died.

"James Lee's Wife" is a series of monologues in which an increasingly lonely woman observes the breaking up of her marriage, as her husband becomes more and more cold. When it appeared, it was compared to George Meredith's *Modern Love,* which was on the same subject—and which Browning had read. (The condoning of adultery in Meredith's work, incidentally, seems not to have bothered him.) One striking fact about Browning's version is that we see and feel everything from a woman's point of view. Even more striking is the woman's reading a poem that Browning had written years earlier (and published in Fox's *Monthly Repository*). Here is a Browning character criticizing Browning himself—Browning, the inspirational poet, with his "young man's" optimism that delights in change, and in trials and troubles. It all seems hollow to a woman who is, psychologically as well as socially, unable to be aggressive or to relish her own sufferings. The poem ends with James Lee's wife leaving her indifferent husband. The marriage is destroyed.

In several of these poems there is a hint of adultery. Browning's most daring poem, that which shocked his contemporaries the most, dealt with this subject openly. In "The Statue and the Bust," Browning condoned the violation of a cold and loveless marriage. His story is about an unhappy wife and her lover who fail to act—who fail to elope from her Florentine palace as Elizabeth and Robert eloped from the house on Wimpole Street. They are morally condemned for this failure. "The Statue and the Bust" was rightly taken by most of its readers to argue that honest adultery is better than empty marriage.

Again, in *Fifine at the Fair,* about the legendary and notorious Don Juan, Browning made no moral condemnation of philandering. At least, his Don Juan defends his notorious and un-Victorian promiscuity in sophisticated language that sounds like Browning's own—the language used in some of his more personal poetic statements. The point is not that Robert Browning had had sexual relations with women other than his wife or that he expressed both his guilt and his defense in these poems; but he seems to have had the matter on his mind.

Most important, Browning was enough of a rebel against conventional morality to insist on the true sanctions of the heart. In many of the versions he wrote of his and Elizabeth's elopement, he substitutes a husband for the father. The greatest example—his greatest single poem—is *The Ring and the Book.*

Robert and Elizabeth Browning had been living in Florence for thirteen years. He knew its squares, its bridges, its byways. One day in June, 1860, he had been strolling and observing all morning; and about noon he found himself in the Piazza di San Lorenzo, with its bookstalls and little stands that sold reproductions of pictures from the Uffizi and Pitti galleries. In one of the stalls he found an old book that intrigued him, and he bought it —for the equivalent of eightpence. This was the *Old Yellow Book,* and it was the source for his most ambitious and impressive poem. It was a compilation of documents which had to do with a once-famous murder trial, that of Count Guido Franceschini for the murder of his "adulterous wife." Browning took the document with him to Rome, where he and Elizabeth were spending the winter—and so began his masterpiece. *The Ring and the Book,* finally published in 1868 and 1869—after Elizabeth's death—retold the story from the points of view of Roman citizens, of lawyers, and of the Pope (who finally decided the case), as well as of the principals. The latter included Guido, who said he was tricked into marrying young Pompilia by her foster parents, who had given him the impression that she was an heiress; the innocent and bewildered Pompilia, herself a victim

of greed and lies; and Caponsacchi, a canon who, touched by her
beauty and simplicity, helped Pompilia to escape from Guido's
household, which had become a virtual prison.

Although the young wife and the canon were accused of
adultery, Browning makes it clear that they were chaste. So, in
this "novel in verse," as Henry James called it, the escape from
domestic prison differs from Robert's and Elizabeth's elopement;
the liberator is a celibate, not a lover. In other words, the sexual
relationship has become a fetter, and, for Pompilia (she says this
in so many words), escape from sexual duty represents the highest liberation.

The book-length poem is, of course, much more complex
than this brief account indicates. It is, for one thing, the forerun-
ner of modern films like *Rashomon* and works of fiction like
Lawrence Durrell's *Alexandria Quartet,* because it dramatizes
how different one set of events can look when seen through different eyes. But Browning's moral judgment here is lucid enough
as it is summed up by his character of the Pope; and its point is
that Guido's marriage to Pompilia was a lie based on a lie. The
words *divorce* and *adultery* are never used, but it is clear that
Browning believed Pompilia's breaking out of her marriage was
justified.

After Elizabeth Browning's death in 1861, Robert was
briefly—but only briefly—at a loss. He soon reentered social life,
having at last returned to England. He wrote a great deal. In
1871 he proposed to Lady Louise Ashburton, a widow. Apparently he thought she had been encouraging him. Apparently she
had not. It was all rather embarrassing and painful. The aging
poet was especially vexed; but slowly he recovered and even had
later flirtations. His poems and letters make it clear that Browning's vigor and interest in sexual matters hardly waned in his advanced years.

In *Men and Women,* he included an almost startingly sexual piece called "Women and Roses," about women as flowers:

> Dear rose, thy joy's undimmed;
> Thy cup is ruby-rimmed,
> Thy cup's heart nectar-brimmed.

The sexual imagery needs no explicating. Some of his later verse specifies what these lines imply: that he was consistently interested in the physical aspect of sexuality, and—what "The Statue and the Bust" spells out, too—that honesty about sexual passion was more important for him than all the conventions, including that of marriage.

One aspect of Browning's unconventionality was his insistence, both in poetry and in life, upon regarding women not as angels—or as animals—but as people. In spite of the sentimentality of parts of their correspondence, both he and his wife had a clear, cool idea about the value and limitations of human beings, men and women alike. When he was seventy-seven, Browning was infuriated to find in print a private letter written by his old friend Edward FitzGerald about the death of Elizabeth.

> Mrs. Browning's death is rather a relief to me, I must say; no more Aurora Leighs, thank God! A woman of real genius, I know; but what is the upshot of it all? She and her sex had better mind the kitchen and the children; and perhaps the poor.

In his fury, Browning wrote and sent off to be printed a violent sonnet attacking his late friend. His anger was basically personal, of course: he was hurt by the snide remark. But, beyond that— or, rather, as a part of that—it was true that Browning was one of those Victorian men who could respect creative, independent women.

In this, of course, Browning might be said to resemble Mill. It is also a trait he had in common with another eminent Victorian man of letters, the man who—after Mill—came to be the most outstanding champion of women's role and women's rights in the literature of the period: George Meredith.

Meredith and Browning read each other's work, met, and even had a brief correspondence. They were similar in a number of ways. Whether or not Meredith's *Modern Love* inspired Browning to write "James Lee's Wife," both poems display an interest in the psychology of sexual relations and a remarkable realism about the fact, the experience, of marriage. Both men, as it happened, married women six years older than they were. Both were poets with a flair for drama and for novelistic writing. Both were deeply interested in the nature of human sexuality and were willing to countenance, and even to encourage, rebellion against the social conventions that governed marriage and the intercourse between man and woman.

George Meredith was not associated with the London circle that included Fox, the Flower sisters, Mill, and, briefly, Browning. He was born in Portsmouth, where his father was a naval tailor. But, after his father's bankruptcy and removal to London, and after George's two years in a German school, the young man settled down to study law—and write—in London. There he stayed from 1844 to 1849: the last five years of the painful Mill-Taylor triangle, when John Mill and Harriet Taylor had withdrawn from society; and the very years when Robert Browning met, wooed, and at last eloped with, Elizabeth Barrett. Meredith himself met, wooed, and, in 1849, married Mary Ellen Peacock Nicolls. He was twenty-one. She was twenty-eight, a widow with a daughter of five years. She was also—and this may have been an attraction to a young man eager for literary distinction—the daughter of the distinguished writer, Thomas Love Peacock. Unlike Mill's and Browning's experiences, however, this marriage of the young Meredith was a disaster.

From the disaster came Meredith's poetic series entitled *Modern Love*. Other poems, too, and parts and aspects of Meredith's fiction, were influenced by that marriage.

Even more than Harriet Hardy Taylor Mill, Mary Ellen Peacock Nicolls Meredith remains an enigma. She exists for most modern readers—if she exists at all—in an explantory footnote to *Modern Love* or a brief introduction to *The Ordeal of Richard Feverel*. Meredith's biographers are likely to sympathize with his own bitter unhappiness about her and his marriage—or to leave her something of a mystery. (The best life of Meredith, Lionel Stevenson's, tends to skirt the subject.) A recent book about her, Diane Johnson's *Lesser Lives*, portrays her sympathetically as a Victorian rebel against sexual conventions; and there is certainly a good deal of truth in it. Yet, the effect is to cast Meredith as the oppressive Victorian husband, when in fact he was increasingly just such a sexual rebel as his career progressed.

All this is to suggest that Meredith's full response to his unhappy first marriage, and to the dilemma in which both he and his first wife found themselves, was more complex and more long-lasting than some critics think.

George Meredith's introduction to psychosexual problems came earlier than either Mill's or Browning's. When he was only a schoolchild, the housekeeper for his widowed father, that improvident tailor who liked to live as a gentleman, became his father's mistress. The boy probably never approved of this Matilda Buckett, who had no pretensions to being genteel; but he could hardly ignore his father's liaison, especially when that bankrupt father—now in London—actually married the woman. This was 1839, when George was eleven. Five or six years later— so his biographers have guessed—he himself fell in love with a simple country girl, one below the social status he intended to achieve. The story of such a love and its ultimate impossibility appears in a number of his poems and novels.

But it was only after his schooling in Germany—paid for by a small income independent of his father—that he found in the literary world of London the first passions and perplexities that could complicate a frankly sexual nature.

By the time he was eighteen, George Meredith had lost his faith in "the Christian fable" and had begun to formulate his own ideas about physical nature as the basis of man's life. These ideas included a frank recognition that human beings have profound and irrational sexual impulses quite as much as other animals; the point is made repeatedly in Meredith's verse. The extent to which such a theme is intellectual, and the extent to which it represents a personal and passionate nature, is not so clear. But soon after he had succeeded in his wooing of Mrs. Nicolls, and before they were married, a telling incident occurred. (It is, by the way, a scene that may tend to throw doubt on his friends' later assertion that he was inveigled into the engagement—and to support the account more favorable to her that he proposed and was rejected a half-dozen times.) Edith, the five-year-old daughter of the widowed Mary Ellen, came into a darkened room to find the two in an embrace so passionate that it frightened her. Meredith left in confusion, and the child cried, "Mamma, I don't like that man!"

Meredith began his literary career as a poet, and in some

ways his work was always poetic: if one regards imagery, with
symbolic patterns of implication as central to poetry, then he can
fairly be called the most poetic of all English novelists. In any
event, his earliest published verse anticipates something of the
sexual frankness of his novels. Some of it shocked the reviewers.
In 1851, less than two years after his marriage, he published his
first volume of poems and dedicated it "to Thomas Love Peacock, Esq., with the profound admiration and affectionate respect
of his son-in-law." But the poems seem closer to the passionate
nature of Mary Ellen than to that of her satirical, cerebral, and
quintessentially rational father. Although George Eliot's close
friend (soon to be her lover) Henry Lewes admired the poems
in *The Leader*—and both young William Michael Rossetti and
Charles Kingsley were mildly favorable—the reviewer for *The
Guardian* was shocked, declaring that the poet must

> mend his morals and his taste. Coarse sensuality is no proof
> of power, and passionateness and vigour may be attained
> without impurity. Ovid is bad enough, but "Daphne" and
> "The Rape of Aurora" in this volume are worse, from their
> studied and amplified voluptuousness, than anything in the
> Metamorphoses.

One can only guess as to Meredith's reactions; he never took such
harsh criticism easily. But he never changed his basic convictions
—the conviction, for example, that his poem "Daphne" illustrates: that an insistence upon chastity is abnormal and that
voluptuosness is simply a recognition of the natural.

But Meredith wrote about society as well as nature, and he
recognized that in human society the natural sexual impulses can
become complicated. That recognition, certainly, owes a great
deal to his experience of marriage.

For one thing (and one that Meredith's critics have not always recognized), his role as the poet and novelist of the Victorian age who is most sensitive to the plight of the intelligent,
independent woman, is surely related to his having married an
intelligent, independent—if maddening, neurotic, and unfaithful
—woman.

They were in fact a remarkably neurotic couple, both caught
up in an unsatisfactory marriage. Each had strong opinions, and

a vivacious style that seemed easily intolerant if not rude. They were able to admire each other as persons; as husband and wife they were what we would now call incompatible.

Perhaps, increasing the difficulty of reconciling two such temperaments, there were simply too many external elements working against this marriage. Mary Ellen Peacock had managed her father's household (while collaborating with him on a cookbook and some periodical writing), but she had no domestic model, no direct experience of seeing any give-and-take in marriage: since Mary Ellen's childhood, her mother had been insane. Neither husband nor wife, then, was accustomed to conventional Victorian middle-class home life. At the same time, although Peacock disapproved of the marriage and never much liked his son-in-law, the young couple were so poor that they had for a time to live with the old man—until he found the crowded quarters too trying and put them up elsewhere, in a tiny, uncomfortable country house near his. The moves from London to the country and back again were all the more complicated by Mary Ellen's health: her pregnancies were extremely difficult, made worse no doubt by her intense anxiety. To his father-in-law's disgust, Meredith refused to consider giving up a literary career and working in other ways to support a family, even temporarily. (He refused, that is, to make the decision that had been forced upon Robert Browning's father.)

So things went from bad to worse. What had begun (from the slight accounts available) as a reasonably happy relationship involving problems—of money and health as well as personality—was rapidly deteriorating into a state of mutual dissatisfaction, even one of mutual irritation. A sense of this deterioration is what gives virtually a tragic sense to *Modern Love,* Meredith's later account in poetry of these years in his life, of this very "modern" marriage.

Less than five years after they had married, the two were spending as much time apart as they could. When they were alone together they quarrelled. When they were together with guests, at home or dining out, they appeared to be a bright and attractive couple. Certainly, they had good mutual friends. One was an attractive artist, Henry Wallis.

Wallis was a promising pre-Raphaelite painter who became acquainted with the Merediths in the early 1850s when he was fairly young—two years younger than George Meredith, some eight years younger than Mary Ellen. He admired the husband's literary talent, the wife's wit and beauty; his admiration was expressed not only in social intercourse but also in a painting called "Fireside Reverie" that was exhibited in 1855 at the Royal Academy. He used Mary Ellen Meredith as a model for this painting and included in its frame an epigraph (as many Victorian paintings did) consisting of four lines of verse from Meredith himself. Wallis then painted the husband, taking him as the model for what has become his one well-known painting (now in the Tate Gallery, London), "The Death of Chatterton."

While Wallis was doing these paintings and becoming more and more closely acquainted with the family, George Meredith became increasingly aware that the younger man's interest was primarily not in himself but in his wife. Meredith was very often absent from their house—he had taken lodgings in the bohemian Chelsea district of London—so he could hardly pretend to keep close tabs on the ménage in Sussex. By 1858, when Wallis had completed a painting of old Thomas Love Peacock, it was clear what was happening.

Since Meredith and his wife had not had sexual relations for much more than a year, the situation was clear when, in April of 1858, Mary Ellen gave birth to a son. For the occasion she went to the country, to stay with her foster sister near Bristol; and she made no pretense that the child was her husband's, even though he was registered at birth as being the offspring of one "George Meredith, author."

Meredith knew this child was not his and he resented the fact—or at least he felt that the whole situation had become impossible. He would not let his wife return to see their son Arthur, who had been born in 1853, and who was certainly a true and legitimate heir.

Late in 1858, Mary Ellen Meredith and Henry Wallis left together—in effect, eloped—for Capri, already at that point a colony for artists and bohemians. George Meredith was desolate, shamed, bitter. For a period he was so inclined to distrust all women that he engaged a young man to act as a kind of nurse-maid for his five-year-old son.

Much of Meredith's earlier poetry is concerned with the natural force of sex. (Mythological poems like "Daphne" and "The Rape of Aurora" are about the sheer animal sexuality of man and women.) This early poetry deals with the psychology of the sexes and specifically with the natural right of women, supposedly the weaker and lesser sex, to enter fully into the life of any rational society.

Some of these poems may read like sweet, simple Victorian tributes to pure sentiment. The girl described in "Love in the Valley" is compared with flowers, mostly virginal lilies, and the speaker has an ambivalent attitude toward her freedom: his love "would fain keep her changeless;/ Fain would fling the net, and fain have her free." The second line predicts Meredith's imagery in later novels, especially *Diana of the Crossways*, in which marriage is perceived as a trap and the single woman as a hunted creature. There is a more specifically sexual meaning here, however. For her to remain "changeless" would be for this beloved maiden to remain a virgin, and the poet who speaks here wants her to be virginal—she seems "sweeter unpossessed"—even while, paradoxically, he wants to possess her. At least Meredith is presenting here the way in which a widespread Victorian reverence for chastity conflicts with natural desire.

Natural desire is the subject of a good many other poems, in which the parallel is made between animal and vegetable nature on the one hand and human sexual nature on the other. A good example is "Earth and a Wedded Woman," a poem that anticipates attitudes toward sexuality as expressed by D. H. Lawrence: just as the dry earth needs rain, the woman needs the fertilizing force of her absent husband. And in "Margaret's Bridal Eve," the flower images are anything but sentimental: like Tennyson in *Maud*, the poet shifts from a vision of the *maiden* as lily to one of the *woman* as rose; and the traditional meaning of the rose as female sexuality—in fact, as the female sex organs—must have been communicated to the most obtuse and genteel readers. Meredith's refrain in these lines about the bridal eve is, *"There's a rose that's ready for clipping."*

Meredith's mixed reaction to the idea of marriage is suggested repeatedly in these early poems about wedded men and women: marriage recognizes human sexual nature, but it tends to deny individual freedom. In some of his poetry—in "Archduchess Anne," "A Preaching from a Spanish Ballad," "The Nuptials of Attila"—the marriages end in disaster. Other poems —"The Hueless Love," "Union in Disseverance"—show platonic affection between man and woman but no passionate union. In his later poems, as in his novels, Meredith is inclined to stress that men must recognize the rights, the independence, the intelligence of women—if they are to be truly married and not only to possess their wives as objects. But the best-known and most complicated reflection upon marriage is, of course, *Modern Love,* that series of poems inspired specifically by the experience with Mary Ellen and published less than a year after her death in 1861.

She and Wallis had lived barely two years in Italy (their flight there, like the Brownings' elopement, was inspired in large part by her poor health) when she returned to England, a dying woman. Still stung and suffering from her desertion, as he continued to think of it, Meredith refused to see her. *Modern Love,* however, amounts to an attempt to relive and understand the failure of their marriage.

The title is ironic: love, in the marriage described in these verses, is dying or dead. It is "modern" love in that man and wife are intensely self-conscious, analyzing their own feelings—and brooding over failure. Another important point that makes their relationship modern: both husband and wife commit adultery, turning to others for sexual and emotional release and satisfaction. And, far from being condemned, this need is faced honestly; it is the *symptom,* but not at all the *cause,* of their marriage having failed.

Marriage, in *Modern Love,* is called a "wedded lie." But there is a consistent recognition of the irrepressible sexual drive that has led to marriage—and to adultery as well.

This is true even though the poet-speaker is again and again tempted to rail against the woman and her neurotic sensuality, in a way that suggests the madonna-harlot syndrome and Tennyson's railing against feminine sexuality (and sensuality) in *Idylls of the King*. Here is one outburst, when the wife has left the poet —Meredith himself, surely—so that he can go to his mistress:

> Their sense is with their senses all mix'd in,
> Destroyed by subtleties, these women are!
> More brain, O Lord, more brain!

How much "brain" these lines display may be in doubt; and they sound strange coming from the pen of the very man who invented such brainy heroines as Clara Middleton in his later novels. (*Modern Love* was published seventeen years before *The Egoist*.) In fact, one might suspect here the man's ancient tendency to project his own sexual feelings onto the woman—and then to blame her for them. Even so, *Modern Love* tries to be fair to the woman, the wife who is at least as trapped as the husband. The speaker avows his own sexual drive. "What are we first? First, animals," he exclaims. He observes the simple country couple's marriage: "They have the secret of the bull and lamb." And, recognizing the sexual needs of both men and women, he recognizes, too, that it is the combination of natural, imperious sexuality with relentless intellectualizing—with the self-consciously critical mind—that produces the disaster which is "the union of this ever-diverse pair." As hurt as Meredith undoubtedly was by his wife's leaving him for a lover, he was able in this poetry to present her as a human being rather than as a villainous fallen woman. "No villain need be! Passions spin the plot:/ We are betray'd by what is false within."

What is false within is the combination of egoism and yearning for love, of rational coolness and sexual passion that men and women share.

We can only speculate about the full impact of Mary Ellen and unhappy marriage upon Meredith; but his championing of strong and strong-minded women, and indeed of unconventional behavior (including adultery in later novels), must surely be weighed against his refusal to let his wife see their son and his later refusal to see her before she died. Hurt as he was, wounded as his pride was, Meredith did write—concerning the failure of his marriage—that "No villain need be!"

In the poetry that followed *Modern Love* he displayed even more awareness of the woman's plight, not only in modern marriage but also in the modern world. The most striking example is "A Ballad of Fair Ladies in Revolt" (composed, according to G. M. Trevelyan, in 1876). This is an extraordinary poem that might almost be used today as a rallying song for Women's Liberation. It is not a poem of total disillusionment about modern marriage, for the woman speaker says to the two men she encounters, "You have us if you wed our cause." But the speaker is hardly sanguine about marriage as it exists or about the chances for women to be themselves, as wives or in any other role. When young girls come to know men, she declares, "they know the state of war." They learn that they must *use* their beauty—must, in effect, prostitute themselves. And the woman who uses her body in this way, and is so used—the woman who seems to walk "in union" by her husband's side—is, in fact, "a poor slave." This is a total inversion of the sentimental Victorian picture of married life (the vision, for instance, in Tennyson's *The Two Voices*). But the poem goes beyond that.

It answers the ridicule of the philistine male, the man who "speaks the popular voice" and who today might well be called a "male chauvinist pig." He smugly assumes that women's wrongs are rare, that women are, in fact, sheltered from those hardships which men face. Indeed, he says, women live in a kind of Eden. Presumably he is thinking of middle-class and genteel wives and daughters, not the thousands of prostitutes or tens of thousands of shop- and factory-girls. But his interlocutor takes him up on the reference to Eden.

> We are somewhat tired of Eden, is our plea.
> We have thirsted long; this apple suits our drouth:
> 'Tis good for men to halve, think we.

Here is a witty reply to the ages-old misogyny that blames women, Eve in particular, for the fall of mankind; it is also a reply to the newly popular idea that man finds God through prayer and action but woman finds God only in her man. Coventry Patmore would surely have been astonished to think that a woman might "halve" the apple of knowledge. The final question and answer, however, are the most telling. The exasperated male philistine asks, "What seek you?" This is the very question asked today about, among others, blacks and women: "What do they want?" The answer refers, first of all, to those prostitutes who were, for Francis W. Newman, only threats to the moral and physical health of Britain's young men. In the streets of Victorian London—the London of Jack the Ripper—says the articulate "fair lady," "we hear women's shrieks."

> ... And that roar,
> "What seek you?" is of tyrants in all days.
> Sir, get you something of our purity,
> And we will of your strength: we ask no more.

At the end of this dialogue between the witty woman and the obtuse man, the male speaker's more sensitive companion, another man, is persuaded—and goes off with the women. This poem is, at last, an eloquent plea—made by a man who suffered an unhappy marriage with a relatively liberated woman—for the liberation and equality of women.

Meredith's first major novel, *The Ordeal of Richard Feverel,* was patently autobiographical. In it, Sir Austin Feverel is a man embittered about women because his wife has deserted him and run away with her lover, a poet (rather than a painter). But if Sir Austin is a version of the author, so in a sense is his son Richard, whose young love may be a reminiscence of George Meredith's youthful romance. At the same time, this composite character seems in part to project into a fictional future the character of the novelist's young son, Arthur. In several ways, then, the story is not only self-revelation but also self-criticism. For Meredith was aware of his own limitations as an overprotective and yet irritable father bringing up a son (once, when the boy was six, this generally indulgent father became so impatient with Arthur's begging for a sip of wine that he gave him a tumblerfull and made him ill); he said of his Sir Austin that his system for raising a son was wrong because it derived from "wrath at his wife."

Some of Meredith's other work is also biographical and partly autobiographical: the title character in *Evan Harrington* represents the novelist's father, and his grandfather Melchizedec actually appears under his nickname, "the great Mel." But the one recurrent theme in his later novels is perhaps not so obviously personal: it is the subject of marriage—especially how marriage laws and customs affect the independence and happiness of a sensitive, intelligent woman.

George Meredith's experience of marriage was by no means altogether unhappy. Some three years after his first wife's death, he remarried; and by all accounts this second marriage, to Marie Vulliamy, was a placid and successful one. These middle years in Meredith's life, the 1860s and 1870s, were not perfectly idyllic (he worked hard as a reader for the publishing firm of Chapman and Hall, as an essayist and, finally, as a novelist, instead of being able to devote himself to his first love, poetry). But they offered him rewards: friendships with the outstanding literary figures in mid-Victorian London, especially Rossetti and Swinburne; a slowly growing reputation; and, at last, a home and a sense of family. This relative stability may have allowed him to look back calmly on the turbulent earlier years and on the personality and problems of his first wife, to which at last he could do literary justice.

Twenty years after the collapse of his first marriage, Meredith wrote—and in 1879, he published—*The Egoist*, which is still his best-known and most-admired work. This is the first in a series of novels about women and marriage.

Clara Middleton, the heroine of this novel, is seen by her fiancé, Sir Willoughby Patterne, as a pretty object, and is described by his clever woman friend as a "dainty rogue in porcelain"; but she escapes from the egoist Sir Willoughby and from his stifling world of willow-pattern propriety—the world of male egoism and female submissiveness—when she refuses to marry him. The novel ends in a way that is hardly revolutionary: she goes off with the sympathetic Vernon Whitford to the mountains, to marry him. Mountains and fresh air, throughout this novel, seem to symbolize freedom; so the implication may be that it is possible to maintain some freedom, some integrity—even for a woman—within a marriage.

The later novels about women and marriage are *Diana of the Crossways, One of Our Conquerors, Lord Ormont and His*

Aminta, and *The Amazing Marriage.* Of these, *Diana* is the most interesting. In it, Meredith plays with the imagery that Tennyson also evokes (the implications of which he attacks) in *The Princess,* the imagery of the beautiful young woman as a form of game. Men are the hunters, women are the hunted. The ironic truth about the heroine in this novel is, of course, implied by both its title and her name, Diana Merion. She is actually a chaste figure like the goddess but she is also a huntress and not a rabbit or a deer (her suitors think of her as both) : a huntress in the sense of being strong, independent, and actively pursuing her goals in life instead of waiting passively to be wooed, won, owned, tamed, and finally, caged.

Each Meredith heroine refuses, even when caught in the toils of a false and unhappy marriage, to be degraded into a possession. Clara Middleton escapes from her egoist wooer. Diana escapes from a false conception of herself. Aminta, too, at last refuses her proud and selfish Ormont, and Carinthia Jane of *The Amazing Marriage* leaves her proud and arrogant Fleetwood. The only novel in Meredith's "marriage group" that does not quite follow this pattern of the strong woman breaking away from her conventional fetters is *One of Our Conquerors.*

This book, however, might be regarded as Meredith's most shocking—his most radical attack upon the acceptable ideas about the sacredness of marriage. It was published in 1891, five years before Thomas Hardy's *Jude the Obscure* (Meredith had already encouraged Hardy's career as a novelist) ; and it anticipated the later book's sense of how hypocritical society could be about sexual matters—how empty, and worse than empty, the institution of marriage could be. In *One of Our Conquerors* Victor Radnor and Natalia defy convention and live as man and wife, although Victor is already married to an older woman. The results, as in Hardy's *Jude,* are disastrous: their illegitimate daughter is rejected by her fiancé, and both parents suffer. Still, the contrast is clearly made between a merely legal marriage and the psychological and sexual relationship that might be called a true marriage.

Marie Vulliamy Meredith died in 1885, and his son Arthur died in 1890. But George Meredith lived to be an increasingly respected and widely honored literary figure. Late in his life he returned to the writing of poetry, although he was to be known primarily as a novelist. When he died in 1909, permission for the old radical to be buried in Westminster Abbey was refused; he was buried instead in Dorking beside his second wife.

Meredith's influence upon other writers is undeniable. Both as a novelist and as a poet, Thomas Hardy felt it. Of later writers, the one most inclined to follow after him was E. M. Forster. It seems significant that Forster was consistently interested in the liberation of men's and women's sexual behavior. Among his early novels, *The Longest Journey* presents the case for sexual independence as a case against the social necessity of marriage; and *A Room With a View,* which is strikingly Meredithian, concerns a young woman who has to realize her own independence, her own ability to see, to act, to escape from socio-sexual stereotyping. Revolt against any kind of sexual restraint is suggested by the fact that Forster was privately a homosexual and that he also wrote a novel, *Maurice,* on that subject—a novel in which the hero, not unlike Meredith's bold heroines, finally breaks away from social convention and elopes (as did Robert Browning! and Mary Ellen Meredith!) with his lover to Australia. It is also significant that this novel could not be published until after the writer's death. Then, in 1971, it seemed very tame.

But this is another aspect of the subject, which will be covered in a later chapter.

What can we say about these Victorian rebels? About those who fought against a restrictive code of sexuality, who challenged the sanctity of marriage in the interests of individual freedom, especially the freedom of women? Were they so exceptional that they only proved the rule, the general assumption as to what Victorian attitudes toward sexuality were?

In a sense, the answer should be yes. But that answer is unfair to the age. In *any* age, as a matter of fact, the great mass of public opinion, of the not-always-silent majority, is on the side of established repression, of timidity if not enthusiasm for the status quo. What seems striking is the extent to which our modern condemnation of all things Victorian—often associated with

Lytton Strachey in the 1920s—comes directly from the Victorians themselves. Our sense of the smugness, the selfishness, and above all, the prudishness of Victorian men and women was already formulated by what almost every major Victorian writer said: that nineteenth-century England was smug, selfish, and prudish. It was, after all, a time when voices could be raised, *were* raised —and were heard—against the tyranny of what we now call Victorianism.

The times changed rapidly and radically from the 1830s to the 1890s. The late Victorians who began the tradition of sneering at this age—or, at best, of being amused by its quaintness— were themselves thinking of, and sometimes referring specifically to, "the *early* Victorians," with their priggishness, earnestness, and so on. It was much harder to be a rebel against convention, especially against sexual convention, in the 1850s than it was at the end of the century; this is why Browning, to some extent the younger Meredith, and certainly Mill, seem so remarkable. (As we shall see, in her private life, if not in her writing, George Eliot was even more remarkable.)

Not that the successors to Mill and Meredith should be dismissed. Perhaps the late Victorian rebels were bolder because they could more nearly afford to be; yet a novel like Hardy's *Jude the Obscure* and a play like Shaw's *Mrs. Warren's Profession* could still be widely regarded as scandalous near the end of Victoria's long reign.

We have already glanced at Hardy's novel *Jude*, published in 1896, in relation to the work of Meredith. It deserves further comment, however, as perhaps the most shocking major work of this decade. Like Meredith, already established as an eminent man of letters, the fifty-six-year-old Thomas Hardy had produced a half dozen novels, of which two or three were regarded as masterpieces. Among them, only the one preceding *Jude*, the 1891 *Tess of the d'Urbervilles*, might possibly have prepared the genteel late Victorian reader for the bitterness of this last story—and the harshness of its attack upon all kinds of social narrowness and hypocrisy, including prudery and the respect accorded an outworn code of marriage. And *Tess*, concerning the passion and the cruel fate of a woman who could, by the obtuse, be called "fallen," may be taken as more nearly a tragic tale than an indictment of modern society.

Not that *Jude* is a tract. This account of dismal failures in life and love has actually more richness, more reality, than some other Hardy novels—more, certainly, than his many poems about the inevitable death of love in or out of marriage. It was the reality that shocked. That snobbery, that mindless intolerance on the part of university dons which denied Jude the chance to fulfill his one ambition of being a scholar, was still a fact of life. But much worse than this aspect of the story was earthy Arabella's frank use of sex in getting Jude to marry her; the casual way in which marriage could be ignored by country people; and, worst of all, Sue Bridehead's refusal, after both she and Jude have been divorced, to marry again. When a landlady asks Sue if she and Jude are married, Sue replies honestly that they are not—in the sense the woman means (the implication is that they are married in a truer sense). As a result, they are refused lodging, and this refusal is one link in a chain of mean rebuffs that leads to the climax of their children's deaths and their ultimate misery. Finally, the novel relates sex and religion: Sue's refusal of the marriage sacrament is a sign of her honesty in a world where the clerical establishment (including the university) is a mainstay of hypocrisy and repression; her final reverting to guilt-ridden and sex-denying religiosity is a sign not of true conversion but of collapse.

If Hardy's novel was a shocker, worse was yet to come.

The 1890s are often thought of as a time of decadence. Some of the art and poetry of the time was mannered; the most famous —or infamous—magazine of the decade, *The Yellow Book,* was supposed to be mildly shocking; artists and writers like Aubrey Beardsley and Oscar Wilde cultivated odd ways of dressing and talking. But the novels of the day, those written by Thomas Hardy, the aging George Meredith, and the young George Moore, were anything but dreamily unreal or "aesthetic." Moore's *Esther Waters* (1894), about the seduction of a servant girl, her bastard child, and her reconciliation with her divorced suitor, had a new toughness, a new sense of hard reality. It showed the world as it was and predicted the kind of literature which, in the twentieth century, does not gloss over the physical, social, or psychological truths of human sexuality.

There were, of course, some foreign influences at work. There was the influence of the French novel, and especially of Émile Zola (earlier, the scandalous kind of French writing had been typified in English minds by George Sand), who inspired George Moore. In the drama, a form amazingly ill-represented in this age until the 1890s—Shaw's first volume of plays appeared in 1893; and Wilde's masterpiece, *The Importance of Being Earnest,* dates from 1895—the great foreign influence was to be that of Henrik Ibsen.

George Bernard Shaw's *The Quintessence of Ibsenism* was published in 1891. In it he explored and praised those candid and sometimes fierce views of society that mark Ibsen's great plays of the 1880s and 1890s. One of these was *A Doll's House,* actually performed in Ibsen's Norway in 1879, the play that introduced to the stage his idea of what was to be called—by Shaw and others—"the new woman."

If Ibsen scandalized placid Norwegians with plays about political corruption, the travesty of domestic life, and the facts of venereal disease, Shaw was apparently determined to have just as much impact upon Great Britain at the very end of the Victorian age. One of his earliest plays was about the still sensitive matter of prostitution. In fact, the matter was still so scandalous that although *Mrs. Warren's Profession* was written in 1893 and 1894, it was not permitted to be performed in England until many years later. Its first performance, in 1905, was in New Haven, Connecticut!

Later, we will want to refer again to this remarkable play about the social and economic bases of prostitution. Now, it may be enough to point out that this—as well as other "outrageous" plays by Shaw—is a work directly within the Victorian tradition of moral teaching through literature. All the major writers of the period who were at one time or another, and in one way or another, accused of being totally immoral were actually very conscious moralists. (It is no accident that hypocrisy was a main target of many Victorian writers, since prostitution and pornography were so widely and easily tolerated during most of the century—although criticism of the laws and mores about matters sexual, social, and economic were not always taken lightly.)

For the most part, the Victorian rebellion against sexual repression was—from the late 1830s to the end of the century—a protest against the complex of laws and attitudes that made women virtually objects, to be possessed and exploited. Marriage, in particular, had become an excuse not only for sexual, but also (and not so rarely) for economic, exploitation. Until almost the last decade of the century, a married woman could not legally hold property; everything belonged to her husband. The way in which this exploitation led to prostitution (and in a sense it was prostitution to begin with) fascinated writers who were far from being pornographers.

And that may be, finally, the most interesting fact about the great Victorian rebels against sexual repression and sexual manipulation. John Stuart Mill, Robert Browning, George Meredith—and, after them, George Moore and George Bernard Shaw —were all high-minded, high-principled men. In the best sense of the word, they were true Victorians. They were even "moral" in the popular meaning of that adjective—the meaning we have inherited from the Victorians that limits it to sex. They all believed that sexual intercourse should be an expression deeper and more complex than lust and that in a sexual relationship, human beings should recognize and respect each other's individuality.

All these writers seemed, in some ways and at some times, to justify "living in sin." That is, the legal code that defined sin as the absence of an ecclesiastical or a civil seal and ceremony was less important to these Victorian rebels than the true, personal commitment of person to person.

For at least some of them, too, this was a matter of experience. Certainly, the experiences were widely different: Mill's love for a married woman, Browning's love for an older woman, Meredith's frustrated love for an older woman with whom he seemed, at the last, to be incompatible. Yet each of these writers is a critic of male egoism, of Victorian marriage, of institutionalized hypocrisy about the sexual drive, and above all, of the supposedly Victorian attitude (when in fact, it is still a remarkably prevalent attitude in the twentieth century) that divides women into angels upon pedestals or into creatures lower than men and beasts—that is, prostitutes.

Prostitution is the spectre that haunts a large part of Victorian literature, whether it is the prostitution of the streets or the legalized prostitution of marriage. It is Mill's subject in his early essay on women and marriage and in the influential *Subjection of Women*; for in both Mill recognizes that indissoluble marriage may be for women not only a yoke but also (as Elizabeth Barrett Browning put it) a moral abomination. In a perfectly valid sense it is the subject of Browning's masterpiece, *The Ring and the Book,* in which the heroine Pompilia recognizes that she has been sold into a loveless marriage. In the same sense, it is the subject of Meredith's *The Egoist* and his later novels. And certainly it is Hardy's concern in *Jude.* It remained for Shaw to bring the subject even more into the open by writing not about a woman sold by ceremony but rather about an outright whore and madam.

From the evidence of their own writing, one must assume that Mill, Browning (and his wife), Meredith, and Hardy all would agree with what Shaw wrote in the preface to his 1894 play about this subject, that

> prostitution is caused, not by female depravity and male licentiousness, but simply by underpaying, undervaluing, and overworking women so shamefully that the poorest of them are forced to resort to prostitution to keep body and soul together. Indeed all attractive unpropertied women lose money by being infallibly virtuous or contracting marriages that are not more or less venal. If on the large social scale we get what we call vice instead of what we call virtue it is simply because we are paying more for it.

Victorian rebels against the tyranny of marriage should not be confused with free lovers, even with freethinkers, and certainly not with libertines. The writers we have cited here were idealists of a kind as well as moralists. But, unlike a Carlyle and a Patmore, they would not shut their eyes to moral realities in order to dwell on unrealized ideals. It seems possible that not one of them ever committed adultery, although they all recognized it could be entirely justified. (This is assuming a certain amount of fiction in Meredith's *Modern Love*.) We have to look elsewhere to find the publicly acknowledged practice of the sexual freedom that these writers, in varying degrees, advocated. Certainly, we have to look elsewhere to find the breaking of laws and mores other than the marriage code—to find truly unconventional sexual behavior.

But it has usually been true that society is more horrified by what people advocate than by what they quietly do. Sue, in Hardy's *Jude*, would almost surely have got the lodgings—and got on in life—if she had lied about her technical relationship with Jude (for the landlady cared only about a facade of respectability, not the truth). But Hardy and Browning and Meredith and Mill disliked this kind of lying as much as they disliked the lying that called legalized prostitution "marriage."

They were, in the last analysis, rebels because they were earnest.

3
Victorian
Triangles

I have ... much to thank God for, now and ever ... my Father and Mother; and Wife.

(John Ruskin, 1849)

Assuredly if there be any one subject on which I feel no levity it is that of marriage and the relation of the sexes—if there is any one action or relation of my life which is and always has been profoundly serious, it is my relation to Mr. Lewes.... Light and easily broken ties are what I neither desire theoretically nor could live with practically. Women who are satisfied with such ties do *not* act as I have done—they obtain what they desire and are still invited to dinner.

(George Eliot, 1855)

I find that the skeleton in my domestic closet is becoming a pretty big one.

(Charles Dickens, 1856)

The rose and poppy are her flowers; for where
   Is he not found, O Lilith, whom shed scent
And soft-shed kisses and soft sleep shall snare?

(Dante Gabriel Rossetti, 1868)

Not all Victorians were terribly earnest, but a great many at least wanted to appear that way. Oscar Wilde made fun of the whole idea in his best-known comedy: each of the bright young things, Cecily and Gwendolyn, insisted that the man she married had to be *named* Ernest. It might almost, as Wilde suggested, be a late-Victorian motto: for society at large, whether or not it was a wholly hypocritical society, "the importance of being earnest" could hardly be exaggerated.

There were some who thought themselves devil-may-care adventurers, but not many advertised themselves as rakes. And yet the number of sex scandals involving prominent Victorians—public figures, writers, artists—between the 1840s and the 1870s—is surprising. These scandals were likely to involve adultery (the fashion in scandal did not shift to other sexual matters until after 1880); and they were likely to result from high-mindedness and moral principle, not raffishness or even the desire to shock.

The classic sex dilemma that did shock the public was that

familiar triangle of earnest husband, perplexed wife, and sensitive other woman, *or* perplexed husband, earnest wife, and sensitive lover: the Foxes and Liza Flower, the Taylors and John Mill, the Merediths and Henry Wallis. There were others. Among these other triangular situations involving artists and writers, perhaps none produced such direct and obvious literary results as *The Subjection of Women, Modern Love,* and *The Ordeal of Richard Feverel.* But results they did have—in the writings of John Ruskin, of George Eliot, of Charles Dickens, of Dante Gabriel Rossetti.

These names may seem to be a very mixed bag—a critic, two novelists, and a painter-poet. Each is, however, one of the great names in Victorian literature; and, even more strangely, each was a person involved in a sexual dilemma.

Their triangles were of different kinds. Yet each derived from some special sexual problem or attitude, and all developed in the period from the mid 1840s to the mid 1860s.

First, then, Ruskin. John Ruskin came, like the Foxes, the Taylors, and the Brownings, from a dissenting religious background; his family, like Mill's, was of Scottish origin: indeed, like Mill's, Ruskin's grandfather went from Scotland to England to make his fortune. John James Ruskin, the critic's father, was a successful wine merchant, partner in the still extant firm of (Ruskin and) Domecq.

Young John Ruskin sketched, dabbled in water colors, studied with Copley Fielding, acted as an amateur geologist and biologist on family trips to France and Switzerland, haunted the Dulwich art gallery—his parents moved to Denmark Hill, near Dulwich, when he was twenty—and was generally indulged as an only child by his asocial but doting mother and father. As an adolescent, barely seventeen, he fell in love with Adèle Domecq, the child of his father's partner. This may well have been the emotional turning point in his life; for the frustration of his normal emotions then—when both families firmly disapproved of any attachment—may have contributed to the fixation on young girls that Ruskin had to live with the rest of his long and distinguished life.

Adèle Domecq married someone else. The blow, for young

John Ruskin, was traumatic. He was in his first year as a student at Christ Church, Oxford. And it can hardly have made matters easier that his mother insisted upon going with him when he went to the university; she took lodgings near his to see to it that he was—what? safe from temptations? safe from other Adèles? Apparently she was the strong-minded kind of evangelical Protestant whose relation to her child involved an apron string—more like an umbilical cord—that was stout and could strangle.

When he was twenty-one, Ruskin had a hemorrhage which his medical advisors thought might indicate consumption. His family at once took him to Italy to recuperate; and, although he had another attack in Naples, the time spent there and in Switzerland apparently did the young man some good. One theory is that he would have benefited even more if he could have escaped his ubiquitous parents—that his intermittent bad health had at least something to do with their, and especially his mother's, hovering. But he was to break away from family influence—in matters personal, social, and religious—only much later and with some pain and difficulty.

In 1843, when he was twenty-four, John Ruskin published his first volume of *Modern Painters,* originally planned to justify Joseph Turner as the greatest living artist. Turner may well be, from our point of view, the foremost English painter; but he was also highly regarded at that time, and there seems to have been some question as to whether he required young Ruskin's vigorous defense. At any rate, Turner was more embarrassed than pleased. The later volumes of *Modern Painters* ranged far afield, to consider the art of the world—modern, ancient, Renaissance, and all. Ruskin was also inclined fairly early in his critical career to take up moral, political, and scientific matters—indeed, almost any matters which came to his attention. By 1846, when the second volume of *Modern Painters* appeared, he had achieved a reputation for criticism of art and of society. He was a rising literary star. He was in his late twenties. In the nature of things, it seemed inevitable that he should now begin to think seriously of marriage.

All of John Ruskin's life so far had been spent with his parents—living near London, travelling in Europe, even studying at Oxford. Some dubious results of his being kept so closely reined had already appeared: not only his physical illness but also his attacks of neurotic depression, which were to become worse and worse in his later years. It was part of the pattern that when he considered marrying he discussed the matter with the elder Ruskins; and then, with (if not *upon*) their advice, he proposed to the daughter of family friends.

She was Euphemia Gray, "Effie," a pretty girl of Scottish background and she was nine years younger than her bride-groom-to-be.

Her youth, in fact, may have been what interested Ruskin in the match. He first met Effie Gray when she was thirteen and he was twenty-two. She probably seemed even younger. (When she was twenty and a bride, she looked hardly more than a little girl.) At any rate, he composed a fairy tale for her, published as *The King of the Golden River*. The printed "advertisement," or preface, to this slight but mildly amusing tale notes only that it was "written in 1841, at the request of a very young lady." Inevitably, one is reminded of "Lewis Carroll," Charles Dodgson, who later wrote the *Alice* books for pretty ten-year-old Alice Liddell— again with no idea, originally, of their being published. The parallel is a fair one for several reasons. Like Dodgson, of course, Ruskin was deeply attracted only to young girls; that fixation would become increasingly apparent as he grew older. In fact (and this is the interesting point), he was later to be fascinated by the younger sister of that very Alice Liddell who inspired the *Wonderland* and *Looking-Glass* worlds. Some half-dozen years after *Wonderland,* and while the *Looking-Glass* story was being written, Ruskin was in Oxford as Slade Professor of Fine Art. He was fifty, Alice Liddell was fifteen or sixteen, her sister Edith barely thirteen. Inevitably, he was more interested in the younger girl (although both Florence Lennon, in her biography of *Lewis Carroll,* and Martin Gardner, in his *Annotated Alice,* mistakenly suggest that Alice was the object of Ruskin's, as of Dodgson's, attentions). Invited to tea with the two girls—the elder, Alice, arranged the invitation—he was so entranced by the thirteen-year-old that he could not recall later who else was there. Years later, in his autobiography, Ruskin wrote that he could never remember or pay attention to others when Edith was present.

Ruskin's exclusive interest in young girls inevitably raises some psychosexual questions, especially now that we are accustomed by such works as Nabokov's *Lolita* to the idea of explicit sexual relations between a middle-aged man and a girl hardly more than a child. The reasons for this interest almost certainly have to do with a nineteenth-century insistence on female chastity: girls of thirteen could rarely be thought of as seductive, as *femmes fatales*. As to the next question—did either Dodgson's or Ruskin's interest ever extend to more than flirtation over a teacup?—the answer is almost surely negative.

That answer is indicated by the facts of Ruskin's marriage—if "marriage" it can be called.

John Ruskin and Effie Gray were married in 1848, when he was twenty-nine and she was twenty. Childlike in appearance and manner—for some time he thought she was actually a year younger than she was—Effie had wit, even sophistication. Though Victorian young ladies were supposed to know nothing about sex until after marriage, and many of them did know nothing, she must have been puzzled when, immediately after the wedding ceremony, her groom told her that their marriage would involve no physical consummation: no sex at all!

For John Ruskin as he approached thirty, the idea of sexually sullying a young girl would no doubt have been shocking. For his bride, the whole matter was apparently mysterious; and yet she had a sense, a sense that grew in the next few years, that something was strange about their marriage, that something was wrong.

As time went by, Effie came to realize that her husband's parents treated him like a child—a precocious, indeed a brilliant child—and that he in turn felt less interest in her as she came to seem less a child and more a woman.

Besides, she wanted to *have* children, not to nourish a childlike husband or to be treated like a child.

The constant intervention of the elder Ruskins in this marriage-in-name-only was a disastrous and yet inescapable fact, from

Effie's point of view. It was as if she might have been able to seduce her husband—he was still fairly young, good-looking, and very much susceptible to female beauty—in the absence of his dour Scottish father and, above all, of his stern, forbidding mother. But the Ruskins, *père et mère*, were not to be eluded.

Nothing happened. Effie had headaches, talked of babies, but was too timid and too frightened of her mother-in-law to complain.

The modern reader is likely to ask, why did Ruskin marry? Holman Hunt, the moralistic but, for all that, sexually normal painter, believed and perpetuated a story that his parents had persuaded him to make the match and that the sensitive John Ruskin was reluctant. But it now seems clear that he was actually eager to live with Effie. He was genuinely drawn to her prettiness, her youth, her ingenuous manner. Was he impotent? Again the answer is no; he was simply the extreme example of the fastidious Victorian—not mean, not hypocritical, but moral to the very marrow of his bones—who was aware of sexual exploitation, was high-minded, was deeply concerned with the beauty of innocence, and who could not reconcile the spiritual, the ideal, with the physical, the sexual. For him, very young girls were both sexually attractive and sexually untouchable. To his morbidly puritan temperament a consummated marriage would actually have meant living in sin.

Whatever fantasies went along with it, Ruskin's only sexual outlet was masturbation. At least, that was apparently the point of his rather surprising comment in a letter to Mrs. Cowper Temple: "Have I not often told you that I was another Rousseau?" (Rousseau seems to have been best-known to some Victorians as a masturbator, having cheerfully admitted to the practice in his autobiography.) Here is another example of an eminent Victorian—and earnest moralist—being startlingly frank on a sexual matter about which we might expect distinct reticence.

Effie Gray Ruskin grew up, as girls will. The "marriage" became more and more difficult for her. But, often alone, she tried to avoid the flirtations, the temptations, that inevitably offered themselves. She tried, that is, until 1851, when she met John Everett Millais.

John Ruskin had defended Millais and his fellow pre-Raphaelite painter Holman Hunt against the general hostility of the artistic and literary world in his pamphlet *Pre-Raphaelitism*. The grateful artist managed to meet the eminent critic in order to thank him. Soon he became a frequent visitor to the Ruskin house, where the older man was flattered by his respectful attentions and the young wife was pleased when, struck by her beauty, he asked her to pose for him.

Millais was a promising young painter, soon to be one of England's most celebrated and most highly paid members of the Royal Academy. He was also an eager, idealistic, and attractive young man. He had an eye for female beauty, beauty like Effie's. And he was unmarried.

In the summer of 1853 the Ruskins, John and Effie, went for a working holiday to Scotland. Millais went with them.

There, at Glenfinlas, Effie had a blessed escape for the moment from her haughty father-in-law and her cold, suspicious mother-in-law. There the young artist painted his now celebrated Glenfinlas portrait of Ruskin standing beside a rushing mountain stream. There, too, Millais became aware that he was falling in love with Ruskin's wife.

She was still Mrs. Ruskin to him, not even Euphemia. They were polite and proper. Ruskin, always absorbed in his writing and his close observation of the landscape—at times he was as much geologist as art critic—almost ignored the two of them. But even he gradually became aware that something was happening in their household.

The emotional triangle developed rapidly in that strange household of neurotic husband, virgin wife, and eager young guest. Ruskin alternately paid no attention to his puzzled wife and taunted her, half jokingly, about her new admirer. She was not amused. She was, in fact, suffering from ignorance and uncertainty: what did the painter's attentions mean? What was missing from her marriage?

Finally, late in 1853, the unwed wife told her family and

friends the truth—and began proceedings for an annulment.
That annulment was granted in 1854 to "Euphemia Chalmers
Gray, falsely called Ruskin."

John Everett Millais was standing by all this time. Possibly
he had in the meantime given her some experience of what marriage might mean. But that can be only a matter of speculation.
In any event, she married him in 1855.

Effie and Millais had eight children. Ruskin never remarried.

But the great art critic certainly felt some kind of attraction
and desire. He was deeply interested in Dante Gabriel Rossetti's
wife—of whom, more later—and, in 1858, already close to his
fortieth birthday, he met and fell in love with a girl with the
improbable name of Rose La Touche. She was to be the love,
and in a sense the bane, of his later life.

As John Ruskin aged, his taste in girls seemed to be for the
younger and younger. Adèle had been sixteen when he fell in
love with her; Effie had been thirteen when he first met and was
entranced by her; Rose was nine.

The middle-aged man and the child were soon calling each
other by pet names. She was his "Rosie-Posie" and he was her
"St. Crumpet"; they exchanged notes that might be considered
love letters of a sort. It was all very curious.

In fact, it was a flirtation. For Ruskin, it was more than that.
He knew that it was. And so did she.

Rose La Touche was, evidently, an extraordinary child. She
was a beauty, no doubt, but her letters to her very much older
lover indicate a sophistication sometimes rather startling. One of
these, printed *in toto* in Ruskin's autobiographical *Praeterita*, is
especially revealing.

> Dearest St. Crumpet,—I am so sorry—I *couldn't* write be-
> fore, there wasn't one bit of time—I am so sorry you were
> dissappointed—I only got your letter yesterday (Sunday) , &
> we only got to Nice late on Saturday afternoon—So I have
> got up so early this morning to try & get a clear hour before
> breakfast to write to you, which you see I'm doing—So you
> thought of us, dear St. Crumpet, & we too thought so much
> of you—Thank you very much for the Diary letter; it was
> so nice of you to write so long a one—I have so much to

tell you too Archigosauros so I will begin from **Dover**, &
tell what befel us up to Nice—Emily asks me to say that she
did a picture at Dover of Dover Castle in a fog—I think it
was to please you—Well we had a roughish passage, but we
sat on deck & didn't mind—We thought & talked about you—
Every great wave that came we called a ninth wave and we
thought how pleasant it wd be to sit in a storm and draw
them, but I think if you had wanted it done I'd have tryed
to do it St. Crumpet. . . .

The letter proceeds to discuss the Titians and the Veroneses in
the Louvre. And it introduces, startlingly, a sexual response. "Is
it wrong St. Crumpet to like that noble Venus Victrix as well as
Titian If it is, am I a hardened little sinner? Oh, but they are so
beautiful those statues there's one of a Venus leaning against a
tree with a Lacerta running up it."

So she goes on, telling her admirer not to sulk, referring to a
poem by Elizabeth Browning, describing buildings, flowers,
fields; and ending,

I hope Mr and Mrs Ruskin are well now. Will you give
them our love please & take for yourself as much as ever you
please. It will be a great deal if you deign to take all we
send you. I like Nice but I don't much like being trans-
planted except going home. I am ever your rose.

This from a girl hardly ten years old!

At that point Ruskin had known the La Touche family
about a year. The mother, who herself seems rather to have
flirted with him, persuaded the great man to come to their London house and give drawing lessons to her daughters Emily and
Rose; or, rather, the charm of Rose persuaded him. Here is how
he recalls her on their first meeting (less than a year before that
letter, written during the family's French and Italian summer,
that shows the teacher and taught already on such intimate
terms) :

Nine years old on 3d January, 1858, thus now rising toward
ten; neither tall nor short for her age; a little stiff in her
way of standing. The eyes rather deep blue at that time,
and fuller and softer than afterward. Lips perfectly lovely
in profile; a little too wide, and hard in edge, seen in front,
the rest of the features what a fair, well-bred Irish girl's
usually are; the hair, perhaps, more graceful in short curls

round the forehead, and softer than one sees often, in the
close-bound tresses above the neck.

The picture, the girl, was to haunt Ruskin always.

From the late 1850s until the late 1870s, Ruskin busied himself with writing, travelling, (and) teaching. His reputation grew.
Early in this period he began to be interested in economics as a
matter of moral concern: his "Political Economy of Art" (published also as *A Joy for Ever*) was a first attack on laissez-faire
theories, an attack that marked the beginning of his breaking
away from parental doctrine (his father was horrified) on matters social, political, and religious. All the while he was corre-
sponding with Rosie-Posie, seeing her whenever he could. He
had, still, an eye for other little girls; he liked to spend as much
time as possible visiting Miss Bell's School for Girls in Cheshire,
where he talked both formally and informally with the very
young students, and his *Ethics of the Dust* began with some of
these talks. But Rose La Touche was never out of his mind.
When she was sixteen, he proposed to her parents that she marry
him.

Accounts of their reaction vary, but the bustling Mrs. La
Touche seems not to have been so shocked as some reports suggest. Even though the disparity of age between forty-six and sixteen may appear great, the idea was taken seriously.

But it was scotched—by Effie. When the La Touches asked
her about the circumstances of her "marriage" to John Ruskin,
she wrote a reply that made clear the sexual oddity of Ruskin as
well as the interfering nature of those aging parents who still
treated him like a child. She urged that the relations between the
older man and young Rose be broken off. And they were.

After that, even correspondence between the two was dis-
couraged. The frustrated middle-aged lover fell into a state of depression, depression that was to plague him intermittently for the
rest of his life. What may seem more remarkable, young Rose La
Touche was affected in much the same way.

In some sense, Rose was in love with the relatively elderly
man with whom she had flirted for so long and charmed so
much. Soon after her parents insisted that she give him up, she
fell seriously ill, both physically and mentally. She lost weight;

she began to lose her delicate good looks. Always sensitive and inclined to be hysterical, she suffered periods of actual madness—periods that became more and more frequent. She died, insane, in 1875, at the age of twenty-six.

John Ruskin's father had died in 1864, and the son's grief and guilt—he had increasingly disagreed with the Whiggish old wine merchant on affairs political and social—threw him into deep depression. His mother died in 1871, leaving him alone with a terrible sense of personal tragedy. But Rose's death was the worst of all. It was very nearly, for him, the final blow.

He was surrounded by honors. He was Slade Professor of Art at Oxford. He was recognized as the foremost art critic in the English-speaking world, possibly in the whole world. His influence was enormous. In spite of his crotchets and inconsistencies, that influence seems even greater and Ruskin's genius even more impressive from the point of view of the twentieth century. Such different men as Marcel Proust, Mohandas Gandhi, and Frank Lloyd Wright have acknowledged him as their master (who else in the world could be credited with such diverse disciples, each himself a great genius?). And his stature as a moralist, a fierce opponent of crass capitalism, and an advocate of humanitarian values, appears even higher now than it must have seemed in the latter part of his own century.

He was a bitterly unhappy man.

In 1879 he resigned his Oxford professorship. He began to write letters, pamphlets, articles, and books about the darkening skies and darkening of life throughout the Western world. He was not only depressed but insane for periods—periods that became longer and longer in the 1890s.

He died in 1900.

Kate Millett in her book *Sexual Politics* uses Ruskin as an example to show the mildest and even most attractive presentation of Victorian (and modern) sexual myth, that of stereotyping women as flowers in a garden—lovely, mindless, and without volition. The point is fair. It can, however, be pursued to reflect not only upon the cultural repressiveness of Ruskin's age but also (and here is a matter more poignant) upon the sexual tragedy of John Ruskin's life.

This is a man who was able after years of anxiety and study to shake off the basic puritanism, the Scottish Calvinism, of his rearing and actually to appreciate the beauty of fleshly art—the beauty of Renaissance paintings which revealed and revelled in nudity. This is the man who, possibly struck by the moral principles of Robert Owen, could respond with radical indignation to the Whig theories of economic life that justified—rather, glorified—the sweatshop, child labor, starvation of the poor. The ultimate point, the point at which he could never quite arrive, was the acceptance of women he knew as sexual beings, that is, as human beings instead of angels or goddesses or—more appropriate for him—beautiful children.

Certainly, John Ruskin was a Victorian rebel against social and economic repression. The painful sexual triangle in which he was involved with Effie and the lively, impatient young Millais puzzled him and made him nervous but not autocratic or unfair. It now appears that Ruskin was more than anything else a victim: a victim of his own Presbyterian-style rearing, of his neurotic family, and perhaps, too, of his age.

John Ruskin was a genius and, at the end of his life, a madman. What have these facts to do with what we have called the Victorian sexual revolution? Surely, a great deal.

Ruskin's attitudes toward art, toward women, toward sexuality, toward life in general, were essentially religious—that is to say, moral. And although that may sound mildly comic today, it was neither comic nor trivial in an age when prostitution, either on the streets or within the marriage contract, was a commonplace reality. If Ruskin was naive in his idealism, at least he preferred to think of female sexuality as innocently girlish and not as up for sale. He was wrong. He was foolish. At the last, he was mad. But he was never vicious, and he was never a hypocrite.

One of the extraordinary facts about Victorian responses to human sexuality is that nineteenth-century women writers were likely to be more sophisticated, more aware of what was actually going on in the world than men were.

This was true even when they had to disguise their gender—as the Brontë sisters did, writing under the names of Acton Bell,

Currer Bell, and Ellis Bell—and as Mary Ann Evans did, writing under the name of George Eliot.

She was among the greatest writers of the century, one of the half-dozen greatest novelists in the language, one of the most serious intellectuals of her time or any other. In addition, she was a creator of character and situation who could, and can, stand alongside the masters of fiction in any language, perhaps in any century. She had to use a false name, a man's name, in order to be published at all.

George Eliot was one of Ruskin's early and consistent admirers; she reviewed several volumes of *Modern Painters* enthusiastically, emphasizing the moral importance of Ruskin's insistence upon realistic art, upon truth-telling instead of idealizing. Curiously, but perhaps significantly, he could not reciprocate her feelings. He did not admire her novels or her critiques.

Mary Ann Evans was determined to be neither one of Ruskin's flowers nor a fallen woman. The fact that she published under a man's name—so, of course, did her model, George Sand —was significant; and so was the fact that for all her concern with brave women in a hard world, her works are not as explicitly feminist as the essays of Mill or the novels of Meredith and, later, Hardy. Yet, in her private life, she became the very model of the "new woman" and a major example of moral courage.

Born in the same year, 1819, George Eliot and John Ruskin were both critics of art and society, both moralists. He wanted to keep women in a garden; she saw women as part of the world at large. He feared sexuality. She faced it frankly.

Mary Ann Evans was born in Warwickshire, where her father was an estate agent. Like Browning's and Ruskin's, her religious background was evangelical-Protestant; but, unlike them, she was nominally an Anglican, a member of the established Church of England. The difference tended to make her social standing just a little bit "better" (although there were plenty of rich and even genteel dissenters from the establishment). At any rate, her father was as much concerned with how they appeared to the neighbors as he was with religious faith and religious observations. As a girl, Mary Ann Evans went to several midlands schools, where she learned piety, dressed plainly, and was in general a very earnest, if not rather priggish, young woman.

She also learned French and Italian and started to read books on her own.

When her mother died, she left school and returned to Warwickshire, where her father permitted her to take lessons in German and Latin. By the time she was sixteen, she seemed destined for the life of a bluestocking—a mildly intellectual and very bookish spinster who perhaps would be expected to work as a governess, certainly to do good works, and most certainly to exemplify meek piety. That destiny would have gone along with her remarkably plain appearance.

Photographs and drawings show her as a horse-faced woman, with a long skull, strong chin, and large mouth—in almost every way (the conventional plaiting of her hair might be the one, almost ludicrous, exception) the antithesis of a Victorian heroine. She did not appear—to anyone else or to herself—at all like a coquette or a *femme fatale*.

Yet, although it might be too much to call her the English George Sand, little Mary Ann Evans, plain as an unpainted fence, was to be a bold and scandalous figure in the world of Victorian letters. She had a warm, rich voice, a steady gaze, a poise and self-assurance that, oddly enough, somehow made her extraordinarily attractive—especially to men.

Above all, she had an inquiring mind, one that was open to new and unorthodox ideas—ideas about religion, about philosophy and science, about art and literature, about sex and marriage.

It all began while she was living in Coventry with her widowed father, when she was eighteen. She became acquainted, through family connections, with one Charles Bray, a manufacturer of ribbons, who was also a secularist and philosophical radical in the tradition that produced both Fox and the younger Mill, those so-called "friends of the species." Bray introduced her to a book written by his brother-in-law Charles Hennell. Called *An Inquiry Concerning the Origin of Christianity*, it undermined the whole supernatural ground on which, up to then, the young girl's moral principles had been based. Was it possible that other and earlier religious cults, including fertility cults antedating historical Hebraism, were the major sources for Christian myth and poetry? The question may seem naive to us, but for a brilliant, earnest, and inquisitive young Victorian woman, it was momentous. She was persuaded. She was dismayed. She told her father that she could no longer go to church.

Today, that may seem to be a trivial matter. Then, it was a bombshell.

Old Mr. Evans was horrified. A Tory, a nominally orthodox churchman, he was concerned with what her world and his would say. For months the girl of barely twenty-three and the outraged old man argued. Finally she compromised; she would read what she pleased and think as she pleased so long as she satisfied his sense of propriety by appearing in the parish church on Sundays. It was the last such compromise with the demands of propriety that she would make.

It was characteristic of Mary Ann Evans that she should make a moral issue of so apparently ordinary and conventional a thing as going to church, instead of agreeing at once to do the discreet thing. Later, after her father's death, she would refuse to be hypocritical, conventional, or discreet about her sex life.

The next few years were busy ones for her. She completed a translation from the German of Strauss's *Life of Jesus*; and she absorbed new and radical ideas about politics, economics, social institutions—including the institution of marriage—as well as about religion. She continued to study languages, to read, to write. Her translation of Strauss, published anonymously at first, was widely discussed. Her mind was developing into maturity—and so, one might say, was her spirit.

After she had completed her first effort in translation, she was invited by relatives of the Brays, the Brabants, to visit them in Wiltshire. The idea was that she should continue to work at her German and at the same time study Greek and discuss theology with Brabant. It all seemed reasonable. Brabant, a considerably older man, contemplated producing a book on the origins and illusions of religion. He was a pompous man with some pretensions to wide if not universal knowledge, and the young woman—still in her twenties, still unpublished except anony-

mously as a translator—may for a while have been impressed by
him.

Mrs. Brabant was *not* impressed by Mary Ann Evans—or by
the arrangement. While her aging husband and the young
woman took long walks together in the Wiltshire countryside,
talking about Greek grammar, epistemology, Germanic culture,
and other matters linguistic, philosophical, theological, and
literary, the wife—increasingly left alone and, when not alone,
left out of conversations—grew more and more irritated. In a
word, she was jealous.

So jealous that, long before the visit was to be over, she insisted that the younger woman had to go. Her befuddled husband gave in. Mary Ann Evans went—resentful and hurt not
only by Mrs. Brabant's jealousy but, even more, by the weakness
of the pedantic, would-be scholar. One of the sharpest portraits
in all of her novels, Casaubon in *Middlemarch*—the pretentious,
selfish, elderly pedant—is at least in part a picture of Brabant.

No one but Mrs. Brabant in the Bray-Hennell-Brabant
circle, or among Mary Ann's other friends, believed there were
grounds for the wife's reaction. That is, there were no even
vaguely sexual grounds; this ridiculous triangle existed only in
one person's mind.

Yet Mary Ann Evans seemed destined to be involved in triangles—truly sexual or not, real or largely imagined.

Less than two years after her father's death, she decided to
leave Coventry for London. She was encouraged by the publisher
John Chapman, who suggested that she stay with his family.
There she arrived at the beginning of 1851, to settle in. But it
was not to be for long.

Chapman had published *The Life of Jesus* and was to play
a part in the young writer's career as owner of the *Westminster
Review*—that organ of philosophic radicalism with which John
Stuart Mill had so long been associated as contributor and editor.
The part Chapman played in her life at this point is more ambiguous, perhaps. At any rate, the young woman was once again con-
fronted by a jealous wife. Now, however, the conventional triangle was complicated: it was actually a rectangle!

Before *Marian* Evans (it was at this point that she changed the spelling of her name) arrived at the Chapman house in the Strand, a triangle did indeed exist. The governess for the Chapman children had become their father's mistress. Upon her arrival, then, Marian found not one but two jealous women.

It must have been an extraordinary household. John Chapman must have been an extraordinary man. His diary's frank account of his affairs suggests as much; so do other contemporary comments about his personal magnetism. He had sexual appeal —an appeal that Marian felt, even though there is no evidence that she gave the wife or the mistress any physical grounds for being jealous. One of the mysteries about this situation is why the two women tolerated each other when neither could tolerate the presence of a third. (Was there some affinity between them or did Chapman manage the whole thing with remarkable skill?) Even more intriguing, what was there about Marian, who was so earnest and so ugly, that made her both fascinating and the object of fierce and surprising jealousies?

Perhaps one answer is that she was a woman with a mind and conscience who steadfastly refused to play the stereotyped female role. Not that she was strident, or even as fierce in her independence as Harriet Martineau, that plain and deaf intellectual who was sometimes cruelly caricatured as *the* bluestocking-spinster (although she was respected by the *Westminster* group —including Mill, even when he disagreed with her). But Marian Evans, the George Eliot to be, always had to be herself.

She was sufficiently aware of the atmosphere in that house in the Strand to return to Coventry in a matter of weeks.

Yet it was only a few months before she had returned to London. From 1851 to 1854, she worked with and for Chapman as sub-editor of the *Westminster,* now and then writing articles for the journal.

She even began to visit, on social evenings, the very house from which she had been driven by a concentration of jealousy. In that house, she met some of the great literary figures of the time, and especially those whose views were consistent with the radicalism of the *Westminster.* One of these was Herbert Spencer, sub-editor of *The Economist,* who had already written a book called *Social Statics* that Chapman published. The talk, among those literary people who knew both sub-editors and who frequented the Chapman *salon,* was that Marian Evans and Herbert Spencer either were engaged to be married or had an understanding. They were not, and they did not. *He* makes this clear enough in his *Autobiography*; he simply admired her mind. And it would be difficult to imagine anyone so sensitive and subtle as she was being seriously interested in such a liaison with the downright humorless, straightforward, in some ways admirable, but always obtuse Herbert Spencer. He was an early sociologist. His contribution to the rigid laissez-faire economics that Utilitarians almost all favored (including, for instance, Harriet Martineau) was a series of works so doctrinaire and blind to facts— or, indeed, to the moral exigencies that the Tory Ruskin clearly saw—that he could prefer the enslavement and death of numberless workers and the cruelest forms of child labor to any abrogation of free trade or "free enterprise." (In this respect, it is difficult to keep in mind that for mid-Victorian, British politics the words *liberal* and *radical* connote what would become some of the most extreme right-wing attitudes in modern politics, in America or in Britain.) Herbert Spencer was of her circle but not at all of her mental and moral calibre.

No, Herbert Spencer was not likely to win Marian Evans as a wife. Through him, however, she met the two men who did win her.

First, there was that remarkable Victorian critic, journalist, editor, and political figure, George Henry Lewes.

Born in London almost two years before the woman he was to spend the latter part of his life with, Lewes was a radical of an older school. His family was theatrical—his grandfather was an actor and his father, manager of the Liverpool Theatre Royal. As a young man he tried writing plays and novels. His younger life might be taken as a prediction of some recent sexual experiments. When he was twenty-four, in 1841, he married Agnes Jervis. He and his wife then lived in what could be called a sexual commune, with three other couples. One member of the communal group was Thornton Leigh Hunt; by him Lewes's wife had a child in 1850.

It seems that the first illegitimate child his wife bore to his friend and colleague—he and Hunt had just founded a radical weekly, *The Leader*—did not destroy at least the semblance of a marriage: the child was registered as Edmund Lewes; and all three, husband, wife, and lover, remained on good terms. In this, evidently, Lewes was more tolerant than George Meredith was to be eight years later. (On the other hand, Agnes Lewes had already had three of Lewes's own sons; his was no frigid marriage, no Ruskin-Millais triangle.) But the *ménage à trois* in which all seem to have been at least intermittently involved was awkward for Lewes. At least it came to seem so. By 1851, he had had no intercourse with his wife-in-name for more than a year; and when she had yet another child, there could be no doubt that this, too, was Hunt's. At that point the husband-in-name gave up any hope of continuing even that semblance of a married life.

Lewes, over thirty, was less inclined than he had been at twenty to live a wholly unconventional existence. He was neither inclined to be celibate. But, having acknowledged as his own his wife's first illegitimate child and having patently condoned the relations between her and his friend, he had no chance of suing for divorce. During the 1850s, divorce was difficult enough to obtain in any circumstances. In his circumstances, it was out of the question.

It was at this point that Lewes met Marian Evans. She was sympathetic, an intellectual companion—as Agnes had hardly been—who was interested in his writing, and they belonged to the same circle of political journalists, the *Westminster–Leader* circle.

Soon the two were regularly going together to the plays and operas that he had to review. If he lacked the vigor, the "push," of a Herbert Spencer, he was a much more cultivated man, one with broader and more liberal tastes and one much more to the taste of a woman who, at the age of thirty-two, had no intention of remaining a merely bookish virgin for the rest of her life —or, yet, of throwing herself away.

As she did everything, she made this decision deliberately: upon completing her second important translation from the German—of Feuerbach's *Essence of Christianity*, again published by Chapman—she decided to go to Germany with Lewes, in effect, on a honeymoon! From then on, the two lived together openly in a sexual union that she insisted on regarding as a marriage, not a sacramentally blessed or legally recognized union perhaps but, for her, a spiritual "marriage of true minds."

It was 1854; and in 1854, most middle-class English men and women regarded the relationship of Marian Evans and George Lewes as, indeed, living in sin (they had not even the decency to hide that sin!). For *them*, of course, the hypocrisy of covering up their sexual relationship would be the equivalent of sinning— sinning against the truth, against their own principles. But their openness was an invitation to social disaster. For her it was much more dangerous, much more an act of courage, than for him. She was at the beginning of an intellectual and literary career that just might be blighted by scandal. She had no sympathetic family to protect her. Above all, she was a woman.

Twenty years earlier, John Stuart Mill and Harriet Taylor had suffered for a much less drastic breaking of the social rules: they had no openly avowed sexual relationship, after all; Mill was single; and Harriet had the protection of a home and husband. Still, twenty years may have made some difference. At any rate, Marian Evans regarded Harriet Taylor Mill with respect— as she did Mill. The older woman died four years after the beginning of the Evans-Lewes "marriage," and in 1861, when the couple visited her grave in Avignon, it was like a pilgrimage.

Marian said to her friends, the Brays, that women who were really loose, really sexually immoral, did not behave as she was behaving; they had lovers and were "still invited to dinner." Over the years it became more and more clear that she was anything but a loose or immoral woman. She and Lewes, both working constantly at editing, translating, writing, stayed together until his death.

Lewes devoted himself to his life of Goethe, which was to be one of the great and influential Victorian intellectual biographies. At the same time, however, he had to do periodical writing to support not only himself but also his three sons—at school in Switzerland in the 1850s and 1860s—and, surprisingly, his nominal wife Agnes! Her affair with Hunt continued, and between 1850 and 1857 she bore him four children. Every one of these was registered under the name of Lewes—apparently with the consent of the husband-in-absentia as well as the lover and, presumably, the father of them all. Her whole history is somewhat obscure, but Agnes Jervis Lewes might appear to have succeeded in escaping the common fate, common at least in art and fiction, of the "fallen woman"; that is, she apparently succeeded in having lover and husband, too, along with a family—as Mary Ellen Meredith had not done. Unlike the unconventional and tragic Mary Ellen, the unconventional and complacent Agnes had a long, long life. She died in 1902, supported to the end of her days by a legacy from Lewes.

The unconventional Marian Evans was to have a fairly long life, too, by nineteenth-century standards. For a good part of it, she was known to the public only by her pen name.

"George Eliot" was born in 1858. That was when her book *Scenes of Clerical Life* appeared. First published in *Blackwood's Magazine,* this series of stories used northern English settings and dialect. (*Blackwood's* was a Scottish periodical—it still is—and the book was published in Edinburgh.) It was soon to be followed by *Adam Bede,* really her first novel. This story, too, is set in the northern countryside and makes use of northern dialect. It includes among other memorable characters a Methodist lay preacher, a young woman named Dinah Morris, who appears to represent at least some of the author's own youthful piety and sense of moral responsibility. She is a sympathetic, not a priggish, personality—and the novel ends with her marrying the title character. The other elements in the story are not so cheerful: they include the murder of an illegitimate child by the miserable Hetty Sorrel. The book was indeed somber enough, yet it displayed a sense of humor and—above all—a strikingly new sort of realism. Several critics have observed that it was the equivalent within the novel of that close literal observation which Ruskin had prescribed and the pre-Raphaelite painters had tried to practice.

One after another, her novels followed, novels that established George Eliot as one of the great Victorian masters of fiction: *The Mill on the Floss, Silas Marner, Felix Holt,* her masterpiece *Middlemarch,* and other works of fiction as well as criticism.

In some of these, one can find elements of self-portraiture,

suggestions of how the mature writer remembered and evaluated
her younger self. If Dinah Morris, the lay preacher in *Adam
Bede,* is reminiscent of the Mary Ann Evans who was devoted to
piety and good works, a yet more complicated woman is Gwendolen Harleth in *Daniel Deronda,* the character some readers regard as George Eliot's finest creation. Her fictional life does not
resemble the author's: she marries for money and status, knowing
that her husband Grandcourt is the father of another woman's
children; she suffers from her husband's brutality, to the point of
considering murder; and after Grandcourt's death she is disap-
pointed when the man to whom she is closest, Daniel Deronda
(on discovering his Jewish ancestry), decides to marry someone
else (and devote himself to the cause of a Jewish homeland). But
her movement from youthful self-confidence to greater realism
about the world and herself may parallel the writer's own development. Certainly George Eliot's characterization of the
young Dorothea Brooke in *Middlemarch* makes her sound something like the young Mary Ann.

> Her mind was theoretic, and yearned by its nature after
> some lofty conception of the world . . . she was enamoured
> of intensity . . . likely to seek martyrdom.

Once more, the unhappy marriage of this idealistic young woman
to the self-centered Casaubon helps to mature her.

Whatever the degree of self-revelation in these psychological
portraits, George Eliot's women tend to become realists through
hard experience, and to become realistic in particular about the
often unhappy, even tragic, outcomes of conventional marriage.

If she projected herself and her courage into what she wrote,
it was done subtly. But one can, surely, detect versions of feminine strength defying convention in Gwendolen and, especially,
in Dorothea, the idealistic young woman who discovers the hypocrisies, the deadening conventions, of middle-class, middle-
brow midlands society. She also discovers what it is like to be a
woman in such a society. Her unhappy marriage to the elderly
Casaubon and her later decision as a widow to give up the Casaubon fortune in order to marry Will Ladislaw both make a point.
Even so fine a person as Dorothea, who is certainly one of what

John Stuart Mill calls the "highest of natures" (in *The Subjection of Women*), can suffer from a false and degrading union. The marriage law, the legal right of Casaubon to affect his widow's life from the grave, is set in this book against the freedom of the noble, daring individual, willing to incur punishment for honesty.

For nearly twenty-five years, she and Lewes lived together. They may well have done more than other people in their time to overcome some of the prejudices we think of as Victorian. By the late 1870s, he was respected as an influential essayist and editor; she was already recognized as one of the most impressive novelists of the century. They might still have been considered by many to be living in sin, but she always referred to him as "my husband."

In 1863, they moved to a house in Regent's Park, and it became a center for London literary life, at least for those who were seriously concerned with new ideas and who were at that relatively late date willing to be entertained by an "adulterous" couple. For fifteen years this was a happy, lively home for the two Georges, Eliot and Lewes.

It was in that house, late in November of 1878, that Lewes died.

Much more than his legal widow, George Eliot grieved his loss. For some months, indeed, she would see virtually no one— no one but his son Charles. Now she devoted herself to finishing his work and to honoring him. She herself completed the final volume of his ambitious *Problems of Life and Mind*. She established a fellowship in physiology, in his memory, at Cambridge.

Technically, she had never been married at all—not in the eyes of the church and not in the eyes of the law. (She could not be even a common-law wife; Lewes had been legally married to Agnes throughout these years.) But all of her friends who knew of her complete devotion to George Lewes expected her to be inconsolable—to be in effect a widow for the rest of her life.

Yet she *was* consoled. Again, one has to recognize that this odd woman, plain as she was, had some special personal force as well as that genius which her novels unmistakably display. Less than two years after the death of Lewes she was wooed again.

John Cross, twenty years younger than she was, had been her banker for some time. He had admired her since they first met, years earlier, through Herbert Spencer. Like her, he was recently bereaved (his mother died a week after Lewes). Brought together by mutual grief and sympathy, they married in May of 1880.

Seven months after her first legal marriage at the age of sixty-one, George Eliot died. Her husband, John Cross, memorialized her a few years later in a *Life* drawn largely from her own journals and letters. Since then a number of articles, books, and monographs have been written on her work, especially on her fiction, and she has come to be regarded as one of the great writers of the century. Her greatest memorial is, of course, her work. But her life would be remarkable if she had never published a book or essay—remarkable for courage, for the way she sought and faced the truth, without hypocrisy or fear, whether the matter was one of religion, philosophy, or sex.

Although enthusiasm for the novels of George Eliot diminished generally in the first decades of the twentieth century, there has been a resurgence of interest and of critical acclaim for them during the past twenty years. Some interest in her life as well might be expected today, when we are once again concerned with questions about women in society—and about marriage.

At any rate, her reputation as woman and as artist seems secure (although her reputation in both senses was dubious during much of her life). It may be fair to say that among the mid-Victorian novelists only one other shares with her the very top rank. That one other is Charles Dickens.

Dickens admired the fiction of George Eliot immensely from the beginning. He guessed at once that, in spite of the pseudonym, *Scenes of Clerical Life* was written by a woman. He perceived "such womanly touches" in the book that he wrote to its author

> that the assurance of the title-page is insufficient to satisfy me, even now. If they originated with no woman, I believe that no man ever before had the art of making himself, mentally, so like a woman.

The letter ends by suggesting that she might be his "fellow labourer" and some time later, he wrote to Lewes proposing that she write for his magazine *All the Year Round*. This was after he had learned her sex and her name, which she gave him along with a copy of *Adam Bede*. In fact, the arrangement never came about, but he continued to admire her "noble" work.

The novels of George Eliot are different from those of Dickens in so many respects that we might wonder what he could find in them to admire. Where she was subtle, revealing psychological complexities and moral dilemmas, he was bold to the point of caricature, showing the virtuous and the villainous in melodramatic situations. Yet they did have something in common as writers. Both were concerned with the rigidities of a hypocritical society. Both presented the plight of those relatively powerless, apparently ordinary, people with extraordinary qualities: George Eliot, of women; Dickens, of children.

Both, not incidentally, were aware of what tragic results could follow from an unhappy, a false and yet indissoluble, marriage.

Like George Eliot—and Mill and Meredith—Charles Dickens had reason to know about unhappy marriages. Like the others, he was involved in a Victorian sex triangle, a triangle once more of husband, wife, and other woman.

The early life of Dickens is so well-known that it hardly needs repeating at length; it is also well-known that several of his novels—*David Copperfield* in particular—are versions of their author's childhood. He was born near Portsmouth (George Meredith's birthplace sixteen years later), but by the time he was nine his financially troubled family had settled in a cheap district of London. There, his father was arrested for debt and sent to Marshalsea prison. At the age of ten, Charles went to work in a factory where he put labels on bottles of shoe-blacking. His father, when he got out of prison, became a newspaper reporter; young Charles, although he was then as always interested in the stage, determined to follow the same career—and managed to begin doing so within a few years. First, however, he learned shorthand and supported himself by recording court proceedings, mostly but not entirely in ecclesiastical courts, where he developed that contempt for the letter of the nineteenth-century English law that is so brilliantly displayed in his novel *Bleak House*. At the same time he fell in love.

He was seventeen, she a year older. Her name was Maria Beadnell, and, since her father was in banking, she was socially above the struggling young Dickens. Still, he was attractive and obviously promising, she enjoyed flirting, and there seemed to be some hope for things to come. The hope did not last long. With no family in the proper sense, no money at all, and no great expectations either, he could hardly be considered as a suitor. He never forgot the experience or its moral.

Soon Dickens was writing for various periodicals, including the *Monthly Magazine* and the *Morning Chronicle*—which actually paid him. George Hogarth, the music critic for the *Morning Chronicle*, became editor of its offshoot, the *Evening Chronicle*, when it was founded in 1835; and he asked young Dickens (then twenty-three) to do a series of articles for the new journal. The more or less direct result was Dickens's first book, *Sketches by Boz*. The indirect result was his marriage.

For young Dickens fell in love with Hogarth's even younger daughter Catherine. She was small but buxom, with dark hair, heavy-lidded eyes, a languid manner—in many ways the opposite and complement of the lively young Dickens. The contrast of personalities may have been what attracted both at first as well as what led later on to the disintegration and ultimate failure of their union.

She spoke in baby talk. He wrote to her as "Dearest darling pig." She sometimes sulked because he worked with his pen instead of attending her. He tried to explain: he was a man without means, "doing my best with the stake I have to play for—you and a home for both of us."

In 1836, when he was twenty-four and she was twenty, they were married at St. Luke's Church, Chelsea (where Charles Kingsley was the rector). The ceremony and the breakfast afterward were simple. For a time, theirs was to be a simple household. Charles Dickens was on his way up in the world of literature—but still only on his way.

Sketches by Boz, just published, was a success; yet more was to be done. Dickens was doing it. Days before the wedding ceremony, the first installment of the *Pickwick Papers* appeared. It was to be his first major work and one of his most popular books.

In his middle twenties, Charles Dickens was earning more by his pen than his father had ever done in his clerking and journalism. He was well aware of the fact, and yet somehow never satisfied. True, Catherine proved remarkably fruitful—she had ten children in fifteen years—and he had a household increasingly less small and simple to support. Partly, but only partly, for that reason, he wrote—and wrote—and wrote. From the late 1830s to the late 1850s, he produced some of the best-known and best-loved works of fiction in the English language: *Oliver Twist, Nicholas Nickleby, Barnaby Rudge, Martin Chuzzlewit, Dombey and Son, David Copperfield, Bleak House, Little Dorrit, A Tale of Two Cities.* During these years he became—as novelist, editor, lecturer, and story-teller—a financially successful as well as an immensely popular and critically acclaimed writer. During these years he became more and more lonely, and it was increasingly clear that his marriage to Catherine was a failure.

At first, to be sure, it was a placid, even a quite happy, marriage. By 1840, however, the husband was beginning to be irritated by his wife's lack of wit and style, and then by *her* irritability—which may, after all, have had something to do with his impatience. We cannot entirely sympathize with that impatience. He was moving already in social circles where he was afraid she would never shine. (The point is ironic: her father had been a friend of Sir Walter Scott; *his* father a navy clerk who served time in debtor's prison.) But he was hardly shunning her: she continued to bear him children until 1852.

It may be that Catherine nagged and chattered, even that she was something of a shrew. Critics have suggested that some of Dickens's trying women—almost always, in fact, wives—were versions of his own wife: Mrs. Varden, for example, in *Barnaby Rudge* (published in 1841 and written, therefore, just when the rift between husband and wife was beginning to be apparent). But all the evidence suggests that he was no joy to live with, indeed, that he could be a domestic tyrant. He insisted that she accompany him on his first American tour in 1842, although she was extremely reluctant to leave their children; she went with misgivings, put up with all the discomforts bravely, and by and large conducted herself admirably. She was more than glad when they returned to England.

Soon after their return, however, in 1844, Dickens's unhappiness with his marriage was reflected in his temporary infatuation with a young pianist named, oddly, Christina Weller (oddly because the secondary comic character in the *Pickwick Papers* is, of course, Sam Weller; when Dickens introduced "Miss Weller" to a Liverpool audience, they roared with laughter).

This situation was not improved by the introduction into the Dickens household of Catherine's younger sister Georgina, who tended to irk her brother-in-law, largely because the two sisters at first agreed with each other—and disagreed with him. But that was only at first.

His disillusionment about marriage—reflected in the unhappy marriages of which he wrote in *Dombey and Son* and *David Copperfield*—came to the point, when in 1858, after twenty-two years of living together, Charles and Catherine agreed to a separation. That separation was caused in part, no doubt, by his nervous irritability. It was due in part, also, to her jealousy—jealousy not now wholly unfounded.

Dickens had had a series of flirtations, possibly innocent flirtations, during his years with Catherine. Christina Weller can be safely placed among these. But by 1857, he was ripe for something more. About that time he wrote to his great friend Angela Burdett Coutts, the banking heiress, that

> no two people were ever created, with such an impossibility of interest, sympathy, confidence, sentiment, tender union of any kind between them, as there is between my wife and me.

About that time, too, he met Ellen Ternan.

The last of Dickens's ten children by Catherine had been born five years earlier. "Kate," as he called her now, was in her forties and no longer short and buxom: she was short and fat. She was certainly not, by modern standards, an old woman. But

ten children make a difference. And the blonde, blue-eyed Ellen
Ternan was eighteen. She was lively and clever, while Kate was
awkward (for some reason, that especially bothered Dickens)
and sensible but hardly witty.

Ellen Ternan was one of two daughters—the other was
Maria—of the mildly celebrated Mrs. (Frances) Ternan. All
were actresses. Ellen was the younger of the daughters and the
prettier. Dickens, when he agreed to produce Wilkie Collins's
play, *The Frozen Deep*—he was a close friend of Collins and always loved the theatre—arranged to have all three play in the
Manchester performance. It was the beginning of a relationship
—first professional, then personal, and finally, sexual—that was
to shock London's literary circles and to mark the unmistakable
end of Dickens's marriage.

Catherine Dickens had some grounds for suspicion, grounds
that tended to make their circle of friends sympathize with her,
not him. A bracelet that Dickens had bought for Ellen was mistakenly delivered to her. She was upset, although her husband
pointed out that he had given other such gifts to actors in plays
with which he was associated. Rumor became loud and all the
time grew louder; it now seems likely that Charles Dickens and
Ellen Ternan were widely thought to be lovers some time before
they were in fact.

Edgar Johnson, the most thorough, readable, and reliable of
Dickens's biographers, refused to decide just when the emotional
relationship between the older writer and the younger actress
also became a sexual one. There is no doubt, as he makes clear—
and as all their contemporaries knew—that it was such a liaison.
There is considerable doubt whether a sexual triangle existed before Charles and Catherine actually separated.

Undoubtedly, however, *some* kind of triangle did exist.

Oddly enough, Catherine's younger sister Georgina, who had
at first irked her brother-in-law, was sympathetic to him and to
young Ellen after the estrangement of husband and wife. By the
mid-1860s, quite clearly, with Georgina part of the household at
Gad's Hill—the house near Rochester which Dickens had
dreamed of having since childhood and now *had*—the relationship between Charles and Ellen was established.

It was the talk of literary London. Charles Dickens had not only separated from his wife—that he had long since publicly announced—but he was also in effect living with his mistress.

All the concern, the tenderness, even perhaps the jealous attention, that he had never given to his wife, Dickens lavished upon Ellen.

When he was planning his 1867 tour to America, he arranged to send a telegram through a friend to her—both were at least somewhat discreet—which would contain a code message. "All well" would mean that she should come to join him. "Safe and well" would mean that she should not. She was not asked to come on what was to be his last tour.

To him she was "Nelly." To her he must have been something of a father figure; he was easily old enough to be her father. His daughter Mary, in fact, was a year younger than Ellen.

The attitude of his children toward his mistress is an interesting subject, one upon which Johnson briefly touches. What Mary thought, he writes, is quite unclear; what the other daughter Katey thought is, as he puts it, ambiguous.

Katey started to write a life of her great father and then burned what she had written. Of it, she said, "I told only half the truth . . . and a half-truth is worse than a lie." She wrote also, however, that the relationship between Charles Dickens and Ellen Ternan was "more tragic and far-reaching in its effect . . . than that of Nelson and Lady Hamilton."

What are we to make of this comment? Was the liaison a tragic one for Dickens himself as well as for the young actress?

The answer probably is that, as in so many other Victorian triangles, everyone suffered (and certainly in some ways Dickens did) but that the women—mistress as well as wife, Ellen Ternan as well as Catherine Dickens—suffered most.

For Catherine, the period of uncertainty and frustration had been bad enough—she and her husband had moved into separate bedrooms some time before the open break in 1858—and the gradual reinforcement of her jealous fears was worse. (The fulminations of her mother against Dickens and Ellen had not helped the situation.) The worst of all was the actual separation. She was forced to remain silent when Dickens publicly announced that she was the one who insisted on that separation, although it meant her being cut off not only from her husband but also from her children. One daughter, Mary, sided with Dickens in the breakup, as Georgina Hogarth did. Another daughter, Katey, regularly visited her mother; but when Katey was married in 1860, Catherine Dickens was not invited to the wedding. "Do you think he is sorry for me?" she once asked her daughter, and Katey could only cry, "My poor, poor mother!" Later, when she asked Dickens by letter if he would come to the house in Regent's Park to give her some advice, he refused even to answer. She sent him a farewell note in 1867 (while he was arranging for the code messages from Ellen), and he replied, "I am glad to receive your letter, and to reciprocate your good wishes." They never saw each other again. When he died in 1870 he left her a fair amount of money; the first bequest in his will, however, was not to his wife but to Ellen.

There is evidence that Ellen herself suffered as well. Certainly her reputation suffered. Much as Dickens tried to protect her from scandal, it was inevitable. An indiscreet remark of Thackeray's at the time of the separation did not help. When someone at the Garrick Club told him that Dickens was having an affair with his sister-in-law Georgina, Thackeray blurted out, "No such thing, it's with an actress." Edgar Johnson suggests that Dickens won Ellen finally after a long effort and largely against her will. There is, at any rate, a story told much later by a clergyman to whom Ellen confided after Dickens's death: "I had it from her own lips," he declared, "that she loathed the very thought of the intimacy." Part of her feeling, no doubt, was guilt. She certainly may have felt guilt about the wife who was abandoned in her favor after more than twenty years of marriage, about the children also concerned in the separation, and her liaison with their father. It seems inescapable that she felt sexual guilt. Only a very remarkable woman of her class and background could have failed to be bothered by such guilt in her situation in 1860.

And, while she was no lighthearted flirt, neither was Ellen
Ternan a Harriet Taylor or a George Eliot—or even a Mary
Ellen Meredith or a Janie Morris. She was more passive than ac-
tive, it seems, in the whole affair.

That first bequest to her in Dickens's will was the last, unin-
tentional, slur on her name; by mentioning that name first and
leaving her a thousand pounds he revived the scandal. For virtually the rest of her life she was to be known as the actress who
had been a great man's mistress. In mid- and late-Victorian England it was not necessarily a happy way to be known.

Dickens's own reputation did not suffer. Being a man, he
had to contend with very few snubs of the sort George Eliot experienced. In spite of his unhappiness before and during the
traumatic separation, the main effect of the broken marriage and
the affair may have been on his writing.

He made no effort to hush the separation, to keep it out of
his writing, or to avoid any association of his private life with his
position as writer and editor. Far from it. In the June 12, 1858, issue of his *Household Words*, he published a statement headed
Personal, about "some domestic trouble . . . [that had] lately
been brought to an agreement." He denied that any "anger or
ill-will" was involved and went on in a misguided attempt to
protect Ellen from gossip.

> By some means, arising out of wickedness, or out of folly,
> or out of inconceivable wild chance, or out of all three,
> this trouble has been made the occasion of misrepresenta-
> tions, most grossly false, most monstrous, and most cruel—
> involving, not only me, but innocent persons dear to my
> heart.

The main "innocent person" was of course Ellen; and we cannot
be sure if this virtual denial that they were—at that point—having sexual relations was disingenuous or true. What follows, however, the declaration that his wife had no such suspicions—even
though a tearful Kate agreed to the declaration—was certainly
untrue.

> I most solemnly declare, then—and this I do both in my
> own name and in my wife's name—that all the lately whis-
> pered rumours touching the trouble at which I have

glanced, are false. And that whosoever repeats one of them after this denial, will lie as wilfully and foully as it is possible for any false witness to lie, before Heaven and earth.

Nothing could have been better calculated to keep gossip flying.

Worse was to come. Dickens wrote a letter, much longer than the notice, which he told his manager could be shown to friendly eyes. It was not quite a public letter but it was certainly not private. A newspaper man saw and copied it, and in no time the letter was in the press. In it, Dickens explained that only the presence and remonstrances of Georgina had prevented an earlier separation. He goes on to give an interesting version of events:

> For some years past Mrs. Dickens has been in the habit of representing to me that it would be better for her to go away and live apart; that her always increasing estrangement made a mental disorder under which she sometimes labours—more, that she felt herself unfit for the life she had to lead as my wife and that she would be better away.

Too many people knew that this version was not quite the truth. But if this part of the letter was unfortunate, the rest of it was disastrous. It went on to complain that "wicked persons" had

> coupled with this separation the name of a young lady for whom I have a great attachment and regard. I will not repeat her name—I honour it too much. Upon my soul and honour, there is not on this earth a more virtuous and spotless creature than this young lady. I know her to be as innocent and pure, and as good as my own dear daughters. Further, I am quite sure that Mrs. Dickens, having received this assurance from me, must now believe it, in the respect I know her to have for me, and in the perfect confidence I know her, in her better moments, to repose in my truthfulness.

Again, his version of "Mrs. Dickens" and her attitudes is open to some question. It *was* questioned, privately and publicly, too.

One newspaper, the Liverpool *Mercury,* commented on how "this favourite of the public informs some hundreds of thousands of readers that the wife whom he has vowed to love and cherish has utterly failed to discharge the duties of a mother; and he further hints that her mind is disordered." It went on to say, cuttingly, "If this is 'manly consideration,' we should like to be favoured with a definition of unmanly selfishness and heartlessness." For the writer of that piece, poor Kate became the personification of the woman weak and wronged. There may have been something to be said for his point of view.

The journal *John Bull* was skeptical: "Qui s'excuse, s'accuse." Dickens had, it wrote, "committed a grave mistake in telling his readers how little, after all, he thinks of the marriage tie."

How little *did* he think of the tie? There can be no clear and simple answer to that question, but the novels of Dickens, both those written before and those written after this crisis, give some idea of an answer.

In fairly early novels, Dickens gave some evidence of doubt as to the happiness of conventional marriages. One example has already been given: the Vardens in *Barnaby Rudge.* Perhaps an even more obvious example is in *Dombey and Son,* where the irritability, the nagging jealousy, which poisons and virtually destroys a marriage, is not a wife's at all but a husband's, Dombey's. Walter Houghton cites this fictional marriage along with those of the Lydgates in *Middlemarch,* the Grandcourts in George Eliot's *Daniel Deronda,* and the Barnes Newcomes in Thackeray's *The Newcomes* as instances which "preach the moral . . . that since marriages of convenience issued in personal misery and made one or both partners cruel and selfish and cold, it was both foolish and wrong to marry without love."

That *was* a frequent moral in Victorian literature, in the poetry of, say, Tennyson as well as those novels that show the effects of what was called "mammon marriage." Yet it was not a loveless marriage of convenience from which Dickens suffered—or Meredith or Lewes or many of the other Victorians who became entangled in triangular relations. The "modern love" about which Meredith wrote was to begin with a spontaneous and real love. It was easier, all in all, for Victorian writers to moralize on the widespread wrong of marriage for money than to discuss the problem of love and marriage that went sour and could not—because of social pressure as well as legal difficulties —be dissolved.

Dickens was not for the most part a creator of characters

who were psychologically subtle. But recent critics have found more subtlety just beneath his surfaces than might have been suspected earlier—and sometimes these findings are persuasive. Johnson suggests that the imprisonment of Charles Darnay in *A Tale of Two Cities* and his escape were a fantasy version of the author's own imprisonment in marriage and longed-for escape (he "thought of separation as impossible, of his marriage as an iron-barred and stone-walled misery weighed down with adamantine chains") ; that the seemingly hopeless love of young Pip for Estella in *Great Expectations* may reflect Dickens's seemingly hopeless passion for Ellen; and that Bella in *Our Mutual Friend,* who is loved by the hero but whose apparently mercenary nature must be disproved by a test, is once again a version of Ellen.

Yet one of the striking facts about this man of genius who did not hesitate to make public pronouncements about his marriage difficulties—and, inadvertently but quite inevitably, to raise questions and encourage gossip about his sex life—is that the social problem of sexuality in and out of marriage is hardly dealt with by his novels from 1858 on, the period of the separation from Catherine and the affair with Ellen. He treats the subject most fully—and impressively—in an earlier work, *Bleak House,* which was published in 1852 and 1853.

There, the character of Lady Dedlock represents the novelist's one full realization of a woman with a sexual nature and his one clear and sympathetic portrait of a woman imprisoned by the proprieties of social rank, conventional morality, and marriage. She has had an affair with Captain Hawdon, by whom she had a child—Esther Summerson, the rather insipid heroine of the novel —and when she is threatened with exposure, she runs from home and husband to die, melodramatically but movingly as well, upon her lover's grave. Somehow, in these theatrical circumstances, she manages to be the most sympathetic person in the book.

Why could he not, as it seems, work up much sympathy for his own wife? Catherine was not a heroine of romance; by the late 1850s, evidently, she simply did not have the figure for a tragic character. She was an aging, often silly, often irritable little woman. But, we are told, people tend to fall in love with the same "type" again and again in spite of the lessons which experience is supposed to teach; and, for all her theatrical presence, it seems likely that pretty little Ellen Ternan was just such a passive and dependent personality as Catherine Hogarth had been in 1836.

One can hardly condemn a writer's work on the grounds of his private life, and Dickens's genius as a novelist is not open to question. But his reputation as a humane man was damaged in his time by reports of these sexual complications, by suggestions not simply that he was an adulterer but that he was an impatient adulterer who was less than generous to the mother of his ten children.

Another writer of the period whose reputation was affected by a broken marriage and by his sexual life outside any sanction of marriage was Dante Gabriel Rossetti.

As a very young man, Rossetti was an admirer of Dickens the novelist. As a painter he was reviewed—or, at least, noticed from time to time—by Dickens the journalist. In respect to Rossetti's canvases, and all other pre-Raphaelite works of art, the admiration was not mutual. *Household Words,* which is to say Charles Dickens, repeatedly attacked and ridiculed the new school of painting in the 1850s, even when it annexed to that supposed school artists and works of art that had nothing whatever to do with it.

Just when George Eliot was seconding Ruskin in calling for greater realism of subject matter and style—from painters as well as novelists, in the moral cause of honesty as much as the scientific cause of accuracy—Dickens in his journalism was strenuously and sometimes stridently upholding the old demand for an idealizing of man and nature. His most famous, or infamous, onslaught against pre-Raphaelite realism was the attack on the 1850 painting *Christ in the House of His Parents,* by Millais (who was about to meet Ruskin's "wife"—and woo her), which horrified him by showing Mary as a real woman with gnarled hands. The best-known figure among the self-styled pre-Raphaelites, the young Rossetti came in for his share of ridicule from Dickens's pen. But that was fairly casual. The two men hardly knew each other, for Dickens was not well-acquainted with the younger set of artists (ironically, his daughter Katey married a pre-Raphaelite painter, Charles Allston Collins—that was the wedding to which the bride's mother was not invited). They might seem to have had little in common. But each was an artist, a temperamental, and in some ways, unconventional personality; each became involved in a difficult marriage and in further sexual complications. Significantly, they came together as ardent admirers and visitors of Adah Isaacs Menken, the scandalous horse-riding actress known as "The Naked Lady" who tried to have an affair with Swinburne and who represented to London in the 1860s the epitome of sin, sensationalism, and sex.

Although he was not one of Dickens's cronies, Rossetti was extremely close to other literary men. A poet as much as a painter, he counted among his friends a large number of the important Victorian writers. He actually shared lodgings at one time or another with both George Meredith and Algernon Swinburne. Along with Swinburne, he was attacked in a famous review, "The Fleshly School of Poetry," for writing largely about physical beauty and, by hardly subtle implication, about sexual arousal.

Rossetti's connections not only with Meredith but also with Ruskin—and of course Millais—give a sense that we have come full circle, back to the Victorian art world. We might expect this to be a world more Bohemian than genteel, where poets and painters and even art critics provide an atmosphere less earnest and moral than the one we associate with Mill, George Eliot— and all the others whose interest in sexual liberation was general and abstract as well as personal, and whose lives were anything but hedonistic. We might even expect more fun and less nervousness than we observed in Dickens's affairs. But Rossetti, the self-indulgent and amorous exotic, was still a mid-Victorian. If not so torn by emotional and sexual strains as Ruskin, he was nevertheless a man with problems.

For nineteenth-century England, Dante Rossetti *was* something of an exotic. His distinguished but eccentric father was a political exile from Italy whose life work was a study of Dante designed to prove the *Divine Comedy* an anti-ecclesiastical allegory with an essentially "modern" secularist meaning—just about the opposite of what everyone had, and has, thought it meant. His English mother, oddly, was a pious high-church Anglican. One of his sisters, Maria, became an Anglican nun. Another sister wrote the best body of poetry produced by any English woman. The family collected rare animals: aardvarks, wombats, and all manner of fuzzy, furry things. Christened Gabriel Charles Dante Rossetti, first for his father, second, for Charles Lyell, and third, for his father's favorite poet, the bright older son of the family changed his names around and decided to be both a poet and painter. He became both.

An 1827 self-portrait of the young man—he was nineteen—shows him as remarkably good-looking, with long flowing hair and large luminous eyes. It also shows what later pictures of the mustached and bearded Rossetti do not reveal so clearly, the full and very sensuous lips. The sensuous aspect of his personality—sometimes, in fact, the sensual—was always to be a problem. It was always to stand in contrast, in tension, perhaps at last in conflict, with an other-worldly and idealizing tendency that he shared with his sister Christina and that is expressed in the very early work, both visual and literary, of pre-Raphaelitism.

Today we are likely to associate the term *pre-Raphaelite* with pictures of lush women who have great masses of hair, with extremely rich complex design, with the androgynous figures in sexually ambiguous poses that people the later canvases of Edward Burne-Jones. The original pre-Raphaelites intended something almost exactly the opposite of all this.

It began half-jokingly. A group of young enthusiasts, mostly art students, agreed in 1848 that English painting as represented in the work displayed at the Royal Academy and in the mode of teaching within art schools was dull to say the least. They tended, in the way of bright young men, to think that the arts were in need of a new force. They objected, as art students were likely to object, to the endless copying of masterpieces, and especially of Raphael. And they followed, in their enthusiasm, the already spreading fashion of disparagement for the Italian Renaissance, praise for the medieval or "early Christian" style. In architecture, but in other arts as well, the "Gothic revival" was in high flood, and John Ruskin—whose earlier work consistently attacked the Renaissance and praised the Middle Ages upon moral quite as much as aesthetic grounds—was becoming its Victorian high priest. In other words, there was nothing particularly original about what these young men—Rossetti, Millais, and their fellow art student William Holman Hunt—were thinking and saying.

There was not even anything very clear about it. The idea of art before Raphael, of the late medieval, was just that, an idea. None of them had seen much of any genuine pre-Raphaelite art except in some lithographs of Giotto frescoes. Still, it seemed a good idea.

Dante Rossetti's two important very early paintings suggest by their subject matter and style the power of an idea and also its ambiguity. They are both religious, both versions of the young Mary. The model for Mary in both is the painter's sister, Christina. The first, dated 1849 (with the artist's name and the initials PRB added), is *The Girlhood of Mary Virgin.* Here, St. Mary and St. Anne work on a tapestry while St. Joseph prunes a vine outside, a vine that is rather like a Jesse tree. A baby-angel stands by a lily plant perched on a pile of books, each one of which is labelled with a virtue appropriate to the Virgin. The other picture is *Ecce Ancilla Domini* (probably the best thing Rossetti ever painted) in which the lily in Gabriel's hand—almost an enamelled wand—becomes reversed in the lily on the now completed strip of embroidery. Rossetti wrote a pair of sonnets to match these pictures. Like the paintings, they give the impression of being strained in austerity: the decoration is clear, and clearly symbolic, and the slightly awkward simplicity of syntax—"Gone is a great while, and she/ Dwelt young in Nazareth of Galilee"— is related to the nervous rigidity of the figures in both paintings. But in another sense the poetry is hardly pictorial at all. It is filled with abstract nouns and adjectives compiling all the virtues of Mary. The poet seems to feel that his subject is too holy, too unearthly, to be expressed by the language of the senses.

Yet poetry *and* pictures—certainly, the poetry and picture of "The Blessed Damozel," Rossetti's best-known work—combine the other-worldly matter that the early pre-Raphaelites and especially Holman Hunt demanded with a certain richness, even lushness, of form and color. Here is the paradox not only of pre-Raphaelitism but, and most specifically, of Dante Rossetti's personality: he was at once attracted to some dim ideal of spirituality and to the very real and sensual satisfactions of the flesh. His first, but brief, way of satisfying these apparently conflicting demands was to meet and woo an ethereal-looking—and quite real—young woman. Her name was Elizabeth Siddal.

She worked in a hat shop. Walter Deverell, one of the pre-Raphaelite group and a painter of such extravagant good looks that he appeared to belong in an Italian opera, found her and persuaded her to pose for him. He was surprised to discover that this milliner-model behaved, as he said, "like a lady." Soon his fellow artists got to know her and she was in great demand as a model.

She had pale skin blushing into rose, and golden hair. She was languid, composed, lovely, somewhat enigmatic. Ruskin was to call her "a noble, glorious creature." In 1850 she was barely sixteen, six years younger than young Dante Rossetti. (It was not then considered so young: plenty of married women were sixteen, and there were plenty of prostitutes fifteen and younger.) Soon he was using her as a model; soon he was in love with her.

It was ten years after they met before they married, as it was ten years after they married before he published the poems inspired in part by her—and delayed in publication by her early, heart-breaking death.

One of the important personages for both of them in those first ten years was John Ruskin. Coventry Patmore, who was associated with Rossetti and the other pre-Raphaelites in their short-lived 1850 journal *The Germ* (it lasted through four issues) persuaded Ruskin that they were serious artists—persuaded him in fact to defend these young men against their detractors, as he did in two letters to *The Times*. (This was four years before Patmore's *Angel in the House*, his idealizing of marital sex.) Ruskin's letters were then published as a pamphlet, *Pre-Raphaelitism*, that was to be a bulwark for Rossetti, Millais, and all the others against the universally hostile criticism of the periodicals, such criticism as that produced by Charles Dickens. After all, the bias of these painters and writers was exactly Ruskin's bias, for the medieval and against the Renaissance; and their realism, even literalism, accorded neatly with his—as with George Eliot's —teachings. Soon, as seemed natural, Ruskin became friendly with Rossetti and his favorite model, Elizabeth (now known to the painter and his circle as "Lizzie"), and he grew especially fond of her.

She was a woman now; and yet, well into her twenties, she had some of that simplicity that Ruskin might well associate with innocent girlhood. At any rate, he encouraged her, as Rossetti did, to draw. They both admired her work as one might admire the clever drawings of a child.

Between 1850 and 1860 Dante Rossetti wrote a little, painted a little, made plans—and enjoyed himself. Of all the outstanding artists and writers of the age, probably not one was as lazy, as neurotically lazy perhaps, as Rossetti. In this he made a perfect contrast to the compulsively busy Ruskin, who wrote, who lectured, who travelled and drew and wrote some more. But Ruskin was determined to reform Rossetti, to put him on the right track —and to guide the charming young Lizzie as well.

She aspired to be a painter. Ruskin gave her advice and encouragement. She worried about her poor health. Ruskin, with his connections, had her sent to eminent medical men who reassured her. She was concerned about her relationship with Rossetti, about their future, about marriage. Ruskin gave her sage and considered counsel.

As Rossetti's biographer Oswald Doughty comments, "That so signally unsuccessful a husband as Ruskin should offer marital advice must have appealed to [Rossetti's] ironic humour."

Whatever his advice, and after some years, in fact, after the intimacy between Rossetti and Elizabeth on one side and Ruskin on the other had cooled considerably, Dante Gabriel and Lizzie were married in 1860.

It was not quite, following a ten-year affair, a romantic climax or even a bright beginning. Dante Rossetti was thirty-two, Lizzie Siddal was twenty-seven. He had grown stout and sallow. Never physically strong, she was now virtually an invalid relying on opiates to calm her pain and her nerves. He seeems, in fact, to have thought that she was dying, and perhaps he married her for just that reason, to please her in those last days. Aside from other considerations, he was hardly in the financial situation to support a marriage. For years, along with advice to both, Ruskin had provided money. Now that period was over and that source was just about dried up.

Lizzie, who had been for these years in an uncomfortably ambiguous position as Rossetti's "fair woman," his "Soul's Beauty," but simply, as far as the world was concerned, his model and his mistress, wanted the marriage. But even for her it was no triumph. After a honeymoon in France, during which she was ill, they returned to London, where she was hardly better. There were medical bills on top of domestic bills. Now that she was his absolute responsibility there were fewer flings with, for example, his old mistress, the jolly, plump cockney model Fanny Cornforth, who was the very opposite of Lizzie in her fleshliness, her Rubens-like sexuality; Rossetti addressed her in letters as "Dear Elephant." There was also the pressing necessity to work at his painting. He became more and more dour and restive. And as his mood darkened, so inevitably did Lizzie's.

The Dante Rossetti who never liked exerting himself felt greater pressure now, psychological as well as financial, to follow the example of Ruskin and the precept of Carlyle: *to work.*

For a short time things looked brighter, at least for her. She found that she was pregnant. Janey Morris, the wife of Rossetti's friend, fellow poet, and fellow artist William Morris, was also expecting a child; and the two women became closer in these months of 1861.

Janey's baby was successfully delivered and named Jane Alice. Lizzie's child was born dead.

Always nervous and depressive, she now gave way to hysteria. At her calmest she would brood tragically over an empty cradle. At her worst she was in a state of mental collapse. Her physical illnesses returned. She began increasingly to rely on drugs.

The one Rossetti friend who could help to cheer her was Algernon Swinburne. He admired her poems and drawings; he admired her frail beauty; he was always sympathetic. And his frenetic enthusiasm, his wild Bohemian ways must have been bracing to her. He, if anyone, might draw her out of her morbid state of mind. So it seemed in 1862.

On February 10 of that year, Swinburne dined with the Rossettis, husband and wife, at a restaurant in Leicester Square. She appeared to be in good spirits, wearing her new mantle, looking once more lovely if frail, actually chatting and laughing. Swinburne, in high form, infected both Dante Gabriel and Lizzie with his vitality. All in all, it was a gay, even a gala, evening.

The Rossettis went home early, however; she was tired, perhaps from so much liveliness when her existence was ordinarily so quiet. She went to bed soon after nine o'clock. He went out again.

It may be that Rossetti's later sense of guilt as well as grief about that night had to do with where he went. To a mistress? To a prostitute? The rarely spoken assumption has been that his purpose was sexual.

When he returned just before midnight, he found her unconscious and breathing hard; beside her was an empty vial that had contained tincture of opium. By the time medical help could be summoned it was too late for stomach pump or antidote to save her. She died some time in the morning.

The inquest jury's verdict was that she "accidentally took an overdose of laudanum" and so "accidentally, casually, and by misfortune came to her death." They arrived at that verdict in spite of the large amount of the overdose and the evidence that she had suffered nervous depression since her child was born dead. But the custom at inquests was for the jury to declare death accidental rather than suicidal if there was any room for doubt. And room for doubt there was.

That doubt was always in Rossetti's mind. If his wife's death was not entirely one of "mischance," if it had anything to do with his having left her alone that night, he might feel guilty indeed. There may have been other circumstances, omitted at the inquest and in other accounts, that he could not forget. Swinburne, in a letter at the time, declared that the inquest proved Lizzie's mind had been deranged by illness—"so that the worst chance of all was escaped." That "worst chance of all" was probably the revelation that she had left a note—it referred to her brother and read, "Take care of Harry"—which would indicate that she knew exactly what she was doing. But other accounts of what happened would make things even worse. Years later Oscar Wilde told a different version from ours of that evening: according to him, Lizzie was already under the influence of opium at the restaurant and behaved so badly that Rossetti angrily took, her home; when she asked for yet more, he threw the bottle of laudanum into her hands saying, "There, take the lot." He then left with Swinburne, perhaps to visit one of his mistresses. This story is both late and lurid. But it may be substantially true.

Still, Rossetti for the remainder of his life wrestled with his need to believe that Lizzie's death was accidental and the dread that it was not, that it was largely due to him.

He left their house. He tried to write, to draw, to paint. He fell now deeper into the lethargy toward which he had always been temperamentally inclined. But the most dramatic gesture he made to show his grief was at Lizzie's funeral, where he placed the manuscript volume of his mostly unpublished poetry in the coffin beside her body. It seemed for the moment that not only she but also his past and his poetry were dead.

He relied in this hard time on friends—on the William Morrises but especially on George Meredith and Swinburne. He moved from temporary lodgings to a house in Chelsea. And finally he began painting pictures to pay his debts, even began leading what was for him a normal life, seeing the plump, jolly, and sympathetic Fanny Cornforth—she might steal a little but she was healthy and good fun—as model and, again, as mistress. (Although she was a married woman by now, that hardly bothered her when there was the chance for some jollity and perhaps a bit of extra money.) By the middle of the 1860s, he was—almost surprisingly—a success.

And, at the end of the 1860s, widowed for half a dozen years since his brief marriage, he returned to an earlier love. She was Jane Morris, "Janey," whom he had first known when she modelled for him and for William Morris as young Jane Burden. One story is that Rossetti had proposed to her much earlier but then married Lizzie from a sense of duty; another is that he married Lizzie as a reaction only after Janey had married his close friend. Whatever the truth, it is certain that he was always attracted to this tall and enigmatic woman who appears in so many of his drawings and paintings. She was ten years younger than he (Lizzie had been five years younger). She was dark, in contrast to the fair Lizzie. She was, of course, a mother—a figure, one might say, of fruitfulness—again in contrast to Rossetti's poor dead wife. And she was married to one of Rossetti's closest friends.

Morris, the younger man, had been impressed by Rossetti and the pre-Raphaelitism of *The Germ* when he was a student at Oxford; he and Edward Jones (later Burne-Jones) imitated it in their own short-lived journal, *The Oxford and Cambridge Magazine*. Almost as soon as the two met, they began to exert a mutual influence, and they were destined from then on to be associated with each other. Both admired their model, the young Jane Burden; it may be that Dante Rossetti, her lover, persuaded her as he turned to the frail Elizabeth Siddal to marry Morris. Now, in any event, all that was apparently changed. The Morrises had moved to London, to Bloomsbury. Rossetti and Morris were associated, along with Madox Brown, Burne-Jones, and a few others, in "The Firm"—that is, Morris, Marshall, Faulkner and Company, which produced designs for wallpaper, cloth, and stained-glass windows. So, again, Rossetti and Janey Morris were thrown together.

She was no longer the simple teen-aged girl, the daughter of an Oxford groom, the "stunner" whom Rossetti had discovered ten years earlier. But she was still as enigmatic, as calm and statuesque, in fact as beautiful—and perhaps, if all the pictures of her over the years tell the truth, more beautiful now in her own strange, dark, un-English way. In 1858 Swinburne had been amazed "to think of Morris's having that wonderful and most perfect stunner of his to look at or speak to. The idea of marrying her is insane. To kiss her feet is the utmost men should dream of doing." (But Swinburne had special tastes.) In 1869, Henry James waxed even more rapturous about her:

> *Je n'en reviens pas*—she haunts me still. A figure cut out of a missal—one of Rossetti's or Hunt's pictures—to say this gives but a faint idea of her, because when such an image puts on flesh and blood, it is an apparition of fearful and

wonderful intensity. It's hard to say whether she's a grand
synthesis of all the Preraphaelite pictures ever made—or
they a "keen analysis" of her—whether she's an original or a
copy. In either case she's a wonder.

James went on to describe, somewhat less breathlessly, a woman
in costume "guiltless of hoops (or of anything else I should say)"
who has

> a mass of crisp black hair, heaped into great wavy projec-
> tions on each of her temples, a thin pale face, a pair of
> strange, sad, deep, dark, Swinburnian eyes, with great thick
> black oblique brows, joined in the middle and tucking
> themselves away under her hair, a mouth like the "Oriana"
> in our illustrated Tennyson, a long neck, without any
> collar, and in lieu thereof some dozen strings of outlandish
> beads.

It was now, at the end of the 1860s, that Rossetti began
painting Janey again and writing verse about her as well. She was
at least a major inspiration for him to resume his earlier ambitions, and especially his literary ambitions. He was composing the
final poems for the 1870 publication of his sonnet-sequence "The
House of Life." With the development of this extremely personal, although partly disguised and enigmatic series of poems
upon love and death, spirit and flesh, he came more and more
to regret his gesture of putting the earlier unpublished work in
Lizzie's coffin.

Finally, urged by friends and by his own desire for literary
success—he was already becoming well-established as a painter—
he allowed the coffin to be dug up and the manuscript volume,
somewhat damp and stained, to be taken from beside the corpse.

At this point, while Rossetti composed verse about his inner
conflicts, William Morris was preparing for a journey to Iceland,
where he planned to study and to see the background for the
Norse Eddas in which, with his devotion to medieval lore, he had
now become so fascinated. He was to return in 1871 to find that
his good friend Rossetti had now all but openly become his wife's
lover. It was another curious triangle. Morris's stated view on
marriage was such that he could not react with more than silent
sadness. Many years later he wrote that his ideal marriage would

be one in which a "couple will be *free*." Any marriage without mutual love and mutual agreement, he asserted, would amount to prostitution. This is the point of view of his *News from Nowhere*, his 1891 utopian novel, and of course it is consistent with his latter-day radicalism—not the modified Whiggery of the Mill circle but the socialism that was influenced by the Tory morality of Ruskin and was to influence, and largely form, the thinking of the modern English Labour Party.

In 1870 and 1871, however, this was a matter not of moral theory but of bitter experience. Morris found himself in something of the position of a John Taylor.

Janey, the crucial figure in this triangle, remained inscrutable. Rossetti, to do him justice, appeared to find the situation awkward, even painful—although he was constantly drawn to Janey's dark, strange beauty.

One critical theory about Rossetti's *House of Life* is that it represents his inner conflict, not between loyalty to Morris and love for Janey, but rather, between the memory of Lizzie and his current sexual passion. It certainly is true that here, as in his other poetry and in his painting as well, there is a repeated contrast between the dark lady who is sensual and sexual and the fair lady who is spiritual and often supernatural. The point is worth pursuing. For the moment, however, we can observe that contemporary critics were more struck, more shocked, in fact, by the dark sexual side.

Rossetti's volume of *Poems* was published in 1870. The first responses to it were distinctly favorable. It seemed that finally he had achieved the recognition he longed for in poetry—something he now believed he wanted more than fame as a painter.

The blow fell in 1871. It had actually nothing to do with Rossetti's private life, but he could not dissociate public attacks from personal implications. In the October *Contemporary Review*, there appeared an article entitled "The Fleshly School of Poetry." The main objects of its criticism were Swinburne and Rossetti, to both of whom—as poets—the anonymous critic ascribed a presumably immoral, possibly morbid, preoccupation with the flesh at the expense of the spirit—the never-explicated implication being that they were both compulsively concerned with sex. In fact, the background to this whole attack was one of small-scale literary politics involving one Robert Buchanan's resentments against Swinburne and Dante's brother, the critic William Michael Rossetti, not against Dante Gabriel directly. *His* state of mind at this time was such, however, that he could hardly be rational about the matter—even through the succeeding responses and counter-responses, including his own piece called "The Stealthy School of Criticism."

His guilt about Lizzie's death and his guilt about being the lover of a close friend's wife were both, no doubt, elements in his reaction to the attack and controversy. The conflict between what might be called the fleshly and the unearthly in his poetry suggests a profound inner conflict, one that left him vulnerable. Accidental and, in a sense, trivial as it was, Buchanan's anonymous article so shattered Rossetti that he was never again the same.

It was the beginning, then, of a declining period; at the height of his literary success, when he and his pre-Raphaelitism had become not only acceptable at last but eminently respected and fashionable, he was haunted by regret, by doubt, by a nervous sense of being rejected, by the sense of failure.

The morbidity of this sense, a morbidity almost like that of Lizzie herself in her last years, is repeatedly suggested by the verse of Rossetti's later period; it is anticipated, as a matter of fact, in *The House of Life,* where there is an insistent association of sexual love with death.

This association takes two forms. It can involve the pale and other-worldly woman who holds lilies, who is so ethereal that she may easily rise into sainthood, into Heaven; whether she does or not, she is certainly a virgin. Or it can involve the *femme fatale,* the dark and sexual woman whose very sexuality, like that of Keats's "Belle Dame," implies destructiveness and finally death. One is "Soul's Beauty," the other is "Body's Beauty." One type is represented by the Virgin Mary, the innocent Eve, the Blessed Damozel, and Dante's Beatrice; the other by Venus, Lilith, the classical figure of the prostitute, and Keats's—or Swinburne's—or, for that matter, Coleridge's—vampire woman.

It is not particularly original to suggest that the pale unearthly woman in Rossetti's poetry and paintings is very often a memory, a projection, of his wife Lizzie, while the dark erotic woman is a version of his mistress Janey.

In other words, the sexual and psychological—or one might even say the spiritual—triangle in his own mind and art was not so much a triangle of the living William and Jane Morris and himself as it was a triangle of dead pale wife, live dark mistress, and guilty, agonized self. Rossetti's one recurrent subject, in verse and pictures, is the image of woman. In *The House of Life,* but in most of his other poetry as well, this is quite clear. The most recent book on his poetry lists four "fantasies" about women that can be found in his work. These are, in effect, psycho-sexual types. The first is the saving lady, or Beatrice. He painted Lizzie as Beatrice early in his career. The second is the victim, or Ophelia. Millais painted Lizzie as Ophelia, dying as she drifts down a stream, in perhaps his most famous picture, the one for which she posed by lying in a bathtub. (Her later illnesses may have derived largely from that experience: she was too languid to complain when the water in the tub grew cold; as a result she nearly got pneumonia, and started to rely on opiates for relief.) As saving lady, Lizzie is presumably both wife—saving Dante Gabriel, maybe, from his sexual promiscuity—and angel, at least after her death. As victim, she may be either the long-suffering beloved or, more ominously, the deserted and suicidal figure that Ophelia typifies. The other feminine types or fantasies are the *femme fatale,* or Lilith, and the fallen woman, or Mary Magdalene. The model for Rossetti's pictures of Lilith and the archetypal prostitute (in his picture *Found*) was his earthy mistress Fanny Cornforth. It seems interesting that he did not use Janey Morris for such extreme and obvious images of voluptuousness; but Janey *was* his model for an 1858 drawing of the adulterous Queen Guenivere, a drawing that might almost seem prophetic.

These feminine types can actually be reduced to only two; and those two might almost be identified with the polarities of the "madonna-harlot syndrome" which obliges men Victorian or modern—Tennyson was drawn to it in later poetry, and Norman Mailer is the nearly perfect modern example—to see all women as either divine or disgusting. The implication is that they are either above sex in its usual sordid sense or are mere sex objects.

No doubt Rossetti felt the appeal of this syndrome. Yet his poetry makes clear that he was too humane to type real people in this way—or at least to do so consistently. The most shocking of all his supposedly "fleshly" poems was "Jenny," simply because it was about a prostitute. Again, and as usual, the fact most present in the everyday lives of people, the fact of prostitution on the streets (of London), was the one thing that most readers could not tolerate to see presented to them in cold print. Actually, Rossetti's "Jenny" is one of his least "sexual" poems: the young man who is his speaker is interested in talking with the young prostitute, nothing more, and during the dramatic monologue she is, quite unmolested, sound asleep. Here and in, say, "Rose Mary," Rossetti refuses to type women and instead sees them as human beings caught up in complex situations.

The most striking aspect, however, of his sexual fantasies about women in both verse and painting is that they *all* involve that persistent association that runs through *The House of Life,* that association of sex with death. Here, too, the extremes in Rossetti remind us of the extremes in Tennyson: the pale woman, the lily, perfect chastity, imply death through inaction, complete passivity; the dark woman, the rose, sexuality, imply death through total passion, with its frighteningly destructive possibilities.

Tempting as it is to relate all of his later life to Rossetti's sexual experiences and impulses, the period is, in many ways, obscure. Increasingly he relied on alcohol and drugs. There is no doubt that the shock of Buchanan's "Fleshly School" attack, no matter how stupid it was and how inaccurate, affected his mental and ultimately his physical health. We can guess that all of this had to do with guilt feelings about Lizzie and perhaps also about Janey—and the desolate William Morris—as well. But, finally, we can *only* guess.

Finally, in fact, it is to Rossetti's pictures and poems that we turn to base even our guesses. That Buchanan's attack *was* stupid and inaccurate is clear from a brief look at the poems. What is also clear is Rossetti's life-long conflict betweeen some sort of spiritual and ideal sublimation in art and the normal longings of the flesh that were for him unusually strong. This conflict is reflected in his earliest work, and it is of the very essence of the first pre-Raphaelite work—the written work in *The Germ* as well as pre-Raphaelite paintings of the late 1840s and early 1850s. Rossetti's own youthful pictures, as we have already observed, try to combine the two elements; but almost always the dominant early quality is tightness and what might be called a sexless spirituality. As for his poetry, the most notorious example of supposed "fleshliness"—aside from "Jenny," which is not fleshly at all—is "Silent Noon," a poem that evokes a mood but is hardly very physical. More passionate yet is a sonnet that Rossetti decided not to publish at all, one he called "First Fire":

> This hour be her sweet body all my song,
>   Now the same heart-beat blends her gaze with mine,
>   One parted fire, Love's silent countersign:
> Her arms lie open, throbbing with their throng
> Of confluent pulses, bare and fair and strong:
>   And her deep-freighted lips expect me now,
>   Amid the clustering hair that shrines her brow
> Five kisses broad, her neck ten kisses long.
> Lo, Love! thy heaven of Beauty; where a sun
>   Thou shin'st; and art a white-winged moon to press
>   By hidden paths to every hushed recess;
> Yea, and with sinuous lightnings here anon
> Of passionate change, an instant seen and gone,
>   Shalt light the tumult of this loneliness.

But even here there is less nearly specific and passionate sexuality than we can find in a good many parts of the pious Coventry Patmore's *Unknown Eros*.

The point is that Rossetti had at least a normal sex drive but that he was so sensitive to its implications, morally as well as socially, that he tended to have a morbid nervousness about the fact.

He sent his last *Poems* to Patmore, Meredith, Tennyson, Browning—and Ruskin. He wanted, always, to be recognized as the poet, not only the painter, of human passion. But his final years were spent in anxiety, in depression. He drank. He gave in to his habitual lethargy. And, after a long decline that caused his friends considerable distress, he relaxed enough to speak of his own trials. He told Hall Caine in the last months of his life that he *had* been in love with Jane in 1857, when he felt obligated to become engaged to Lizzie.

At home in Cheyne Walk, in the artistic London area of Chelsea, on Easter day—ironically—of 1882, he died.

John Ruskin, who had been Rossetti's patron, might seem to be almost the exact opposite of him as far as sexual matters go— one wholly inhibited, the other largely free and libidinous. But Ruskin and Rossetti both were in fact deeply affected by the often antisexual forces of their class, their times, their culture.

If Dickens appeared more of a free spirit, that appearance too may be in part illusion. He was certainly worried, as Rossetti was, by sexual guilt—although, perhaps, not as much as Ellen Ternan was.

Of all these major figures in Victorian sex triangles, George Eliot—Mary Ann Evans—was probably the clearest-headed and least guilt-ridden while at the same time she was, possibly *because* she was, the most morally sensitive and thoughtful.

What, if anything, do these triangles prove about the age and the people involved?

First, only that people are people, are just fallible human beings, in any age. But, beyond this truism, that the Victorians who became enmeshed in sexually awkward situations were often bold enough to assert their own needs even while they were sensitive enough to admit their own frustrations.

Some of them were bold—and sensitive—enough to go beyond what we have seen.

The attack upon the sanctity of marriage, the assertion of human rights for married women, took a good deal of courage. It took courage, too, perhaps even more, for a man or a woman— especially a woman—to defy codes and conventions as, for instance, George Eliot did, and to live in what most contemporaries were sure to call sin instead of an honest if unsanctified bond.

But more than courage was called for—it may have been madness, foolhardiness, or downright stupidity—when Victorians openly indulged in forms of sexual behavior that could not possibly be reconciled with law and religion.

The ones who did this were the *really* outrageous Victorians, the Victorians who went further than others had in beginning a sexual revolution.

4
Victorian
Deviants

Where between sleep and life some brief space is,
  With love like gold bound round about the head,
  Sex to sweet sex with lips and limbs is wed,
Turning the fruitful feud of hers and his
To the waste wedlock of a sterile kiss.
                    (Algernon Charles Swinburne, 1866)

My dear Burton
   ...I wish you had been at hand or within reach this year,
to see the missives I got from nameless quarters. One anonymous
letter from Dublin threatened me, if I did not suppress my
book within six weeks from that date, with castration. The
writer, "when I least expected, would waylay me, slip my head
in a bag, and remove the obnoxious organs; he had seen his
gamekeeper do it with cats." This is verbatim, though quoted
from memory, as I bestowed the document on a friend who col-
lects curiosities. I beg to add that my unoffending person is as
yet no worse than it was. This was the greatest spree of all; but
I have had letters and notices sent me (American and British)
by the score, which were only less comic whether they come
from friend or foe.
                    (Algernon Charles Swinburne, 1867)

My dear Swinburne
    ...I cannot tell you what pleasure it will give me to see
something by you on me (that sounds rather improper) and in
print.

(Simeon Solomon, 1871)

In our modern capitals, London, Berlin and Paris for instance, the
vice [pederasty] seems subject to periodical outbreaks. For many
years, also, England sent her pederasts to Italy, and especially to
Naples, whence originated the term, "Il vizio Inglese." It would
be invidious to detail the scandals which of late years have
startled the public in London and Dublin: for these the curious
will consult the police reports.

(Richard Burton, 1885)

My dearest boy,
    This is to assure you of my immortal, my eternal love for you.
Tomorrow all will be over. If prison and dishonour be my
destiny, think that my love for you and this idea, this still more
divine belief, that you love me in return will sustain me in my
unhappiness and will make me capable, I hope, of bearing my
grief most patiently...

(Oscar Wilde, 1895)

By now it should be evident that there was a wide range of Victorian attitudes toward sexual matters—marriage and divorce, adultery and free love. When we go further yet, to consider varieties of so-called deviant sexual behavior, including sadism and masochism as well as pederasty, lesbianism, and (to use an extremely ambiguous word) sodomy, it becomes more difficult to define that range.

These were sensitive subjects indeed, unmentionable in any but the lowest society; if they were referred to at all it was in oblique language, and cautiously. As a result, we find it hard now to distinguish clearly between what people did and what they pretended to be, between what they thought or felt privately and what they uttered publicly.

Clearly enough, however, there was plenty of deviant sexual feeling *and* activity; both the sexual intimacies and the latent sadism of the British public school, for one thing, could hardly fail to have their effect on a good many adult lives. Of course, many condemned themselves and felt profoundly guilty about their own sexual feelings. (It was a homosexual, as we shall see, who prompted the campaign against Richard Burton that was largely based on the explorer's supposed homosexual leanings.) But some, at least, had private opinions very different from the received views about any but the most strictly "normal" kind of sex. Again, there was too much diversity in that complicated age for us to speak of "the Victorian attitude"—even on this point.

Nothing more strikingly demonstrates the complex interrelations of Victorian social life, especially the London lives of artists and writers, than that Dante Gabriel Rossetti, the friend and sometime protégé of that stern moralist John Ruskin, was also such a good friend of Algernon Charles Swinburne. They even lived together for a while—Rossetti with his collection of blue china ware, his models, and his mistresses; Swinburne with his collection of odd friends and his odd ways.

Soon after he burst upon the scene in the mid-1860s, Swinburne became for his contemporaries the very embodiment of debauchery, of sin. He was, to begin with, an atheist (although he remained close to his pious mother, who simply refused to take his atheism seriously) ; he was, from fairly early in his boyhood, a masochist who loved to be whipped by women, by men, by anyone; with his devotion to wine and brandy, he became at last so much addicted to drink that we would now call him an alcoholic. As he presented himself in verse, he was also involved in or fascinated by various sexual deviations—lesbianism and male homosexuality, necrophilia, pederasty, and sadism. All in all, he might appear to have been rather an unsavory character, this wild man whose mid-Victorian soubriquet was "Swineburne"; and yet he knew the most eminent people, dined in the most exalted places, inspired undergraduates to chant his verse in their quadrangles, and was even grudgingly admired by some of those who were most shocked when they read his blasphemies and heard of his antics. Whatever else he was, Swinburne was interesting.

He was also an aristocrat.

He was, in fact, the only aristocrat among the major Victorian writers and artists. His father, from an old Northumberland family, was an admiral; and in those days generals and admirals were not successful career men so much as men of high birth. His mother, Lady Jane Swinburne, was a daughter of the Earl of Ashburnham. Although he was born, almost by chance, in London, he spent his early life on country estates in Northumberland and on the Isle of Wight. He especially loved the island home, where he developed his lifelong passion for the sea.

Following family tradition, he went to school at Eton. There he learned to love the classics, most of all the Greek classics; and he learned to love being whipped. His greatest delight as a schoolboy, apparently, was having his buttocks beaten bloody while his face was saturated with cologne. After that, it hardly seems surprsing that he became absorbed in later life with sadomasochistic sex. His experimentation with such sex may well have begun fairly early, during his three years as an undergraduate at Oxford.

He went to Oxford, to always-fashionable Balliol College, in 1857, when he was twenty. Even though he failed to make a brilliant career there—in fact, he left wthout taking a degree—Swinburne learned a great deal in those years about art and life. He made friends—with his fellow student John Nichol and with the famous Balliol don, the redoubtable Benjamin Jowett—while he read, and wrote, and drank, and played. Just how he played, and how much, we cannot be certain. For some years there has been a recurrent question about his sex life, as to whether it was largely or partly homosexual, or indeed was homosexual at all. This is an unanswerable question. If an answer *could* be found, it would probably begin with the Oxford period.

About his intimate affairs during this period, then, we know very little. The main thing we know is that he was producing his first poetry. He left Oxford in 1860; in that same year he published two verse dramas, *The Queen Mother* and *Rosamond,* the one about Catherine de Medici, the other about "fair Rosamond," mistress of Henry II.

Neither of these blank-verse plays represents him at the height of his poetic powers, although they seem remarkable when we recall that they were written by an undergraduate in his very early twenties. Both of them predict Swinburne's consistent interests, since both center on a woman who is strong and, above all, dangerous. The destructive woman is a recurrent figure in Swinburne; and, as his best recent critic says, the underlying theme in almost all his major poetry is "the association of love with death."

Of course, Rossetti, too, wrote almost exclusively about women and, at least in *The House of Life,* associated love with death; and no doubt there was some mutual influence of these two close friends, these two supposedly "fleshly" poets. But in Swinburne, both subject and point of view are much more likely to be pagan than Christian. And in Swinburne the two aspects of woman, spiritual and sexual, are merged into the single figure of the *femme fatale* who not only is a kind of vampire but also is maternal—in effect, the punishing mother.

The point is clear in his first important poetic work, *Atalanta in Calydon.*

In the five years between the publication of his first plays and *Atalanta,* young Swinburne was getting to know, and be known by, London literary circles while he read and wrote and planned his own career. He met the rich collector of both poets and pornography, Monckton Milnes (later Lord Houghton), and visited Fryston, Milnes's country house, which had become the center of a literary and artistic world, a place where brilliant weekend parties might include a large proportion of the great names in mid-Victorian letters. This was in 1861; soon Swinburne had something of a reputation for his knowledge of writers, ancient and modern, for his critical judgment, and for his promise as a new young poet. At the same time he was beginning to make his reputation as a wild eccentric. With his tiny body and great mane of brilliant red hair, he was a madly energetic and a wholly unpredictable imp who could amaze, amuse, or horrify—horrify, that is, those who were somewhat conventional. Monckton Milnes was amused.

In 1862 Swinburne met George Meredith, and soon they were on close terms. That same year, in fact, Meredith and he both lived with Rossetti in his Chelsea house. It must have been an extraordinary ménage, that household in Cheyne Walk. (It was a neighborhood of artists and writers; the Carlyles lived just around the corner.) Poor Rossetti, still shocked and grieving after his wife's death months earlier; a sober Meredith, whose own estranged wife had died hardly a year before; and wifeless young Swinburne, full of electricity, irrepressible, sometimes alarmingly so! Once he startled Rossetti's guests by sliding down a banister and bursting into the drawing room stark naked.

Soon Swinburne's behavior became alarming in more than a social and conventional sense. His friends suspected that the extreme nervous activity which only heavy drinking could calm was some form of epilepsy. Difficult as he might be to live with, it was not thought safe for him to live alone.

The Rossetti-Meredith-Swinburne household did not, however, last very long. By 1864, Swinburne was traveling in France and Italy, where—at Florence—he met both Mrs. Gaskell (as Elizabeth Cleghorn Gaskell was always known) and the aging Walter Savage Landor, whom he admired all his life. Shortly after his return to London, where he settled into new rooms by himself, he was preparing *Atalanta* for publication. It appeared in 1865.

Not only did *Atalanta* introduce the fatal woman as mother, a figure and a theme that was to appear and reappear throughout his work; it also represented Swinburne at his poetic best. After his twenties, he hardly developed; at least he developed no new ideas or style. *Atalanta* remains his masterpiece.

This book-length poem was read in the 1860s as an imitation of Greek tragedy (it was) ; as a series of extravagant verbal and musical effects (it was); and as a hurling of defiance against the Christian God, in the manner of Shelley's "Prometheus" (again, it was). But the most shocking aspect of the work was its sexuality; and this underlying sexual nature became quite clear only later when the reading public had grown uneasily accustomed to the masochism and morbidity of that impulse that produced a series of destructive females: Dolores, Faustine, Venus, Sappho, and others.

Briefly, *Atalanta* is about a young man Swinburne's age, Meleager, who is equally devoted to two strong women, the chaste warrior Atalanta, and his mother Althea. The women in this drama are distinctly "masculine" according to ordinary stereotyping; the sympathetic men, in the same conventional sense, are "feminine," are relatively modest and docile—*but* not at all cowardly or indecisive.

It all has to do with refuting the "male" idea that females are meant to be sacrifices, giving their blood—their virginity— and that a man who admires a strong woman is a "man grown girl," a man who has become effeminate. It also has to do with conflicting loyalties. When Meleager kills his mother's brothers (who are archetypical "male chauvinist pigs"), the mother decides to let her son die.

Meleager's attitude toward both the woman warrior and his mother is one of awe. Both are regarded as virtually supernatural beings. He describes Atalanta as

> Most fair and fearful, feminine, a god,
> Faultless; whom I that love not, being unlike,
> Fear, and give honour, and choose from all the gods.

And he hails his mother as a holy figure when, near the end of the play, he is dying. Women are not wives or mistresses in this poetic drama, not for Meleager; they are goddesses remote and destructive. Their sexual natures make them sacred, awe-inspiring, dangerous. We can see already the outlines of the fierce woman clad in black leather and brandishing a whip, that woman who is the fantasy fulfillment for a masochist, who entices as a prostitute does and who punishes as a mother does— and perhaps goes further than either would.

Finally, Swinburne's hero is identified with the phallic firebrand: when it burns out he will die. Only as this brand is lit does he come to life and speak passionately. Only when he knows that he is dying does he live intensely.

The pattern of *Atalanta* is the one Swinburne follows for almost the next fifty years in his poetry. A frustrated young man is given to woman-worship. His erotic passion for some queen or goddess, some mother-figure, is unconsummated. In spite of Swinburne's reputation as a lascivious poet, there is practically never any consummated sex in his verse. Frustration and the failure of sex are his specialties.

The date of *Atalanta,* 1865, marks the start of his career—as a personage in English literature and as a scandalous character. But the next year saw the most scandalous of his early publications, the notorious *Poems and Ballads.* This was the volume that horrified the Victorian public with its poems about revolution, sadism, lesbianism, and blasphemy. It was a shocker.

Swinburne had to defend some of these poems—"Anactoria," for one, the lesbian poem in which Sappho speaks as a sadist to the young woman she loves:

> I would my love could kill thee; I am satiated
> With seeing thee live and fain would have thee dead.
> I would earth had thy body as fruit to eat,
> And no mouth but some serpent's found thee sweet.
> I would find grievous ways to have thee slain,
> Intense device, and superflux of pain,
> Vex thee with amorous agonies. . . .

and so she goes on for nearly three hundred lines. The poet's defense of this and other versions of sadomasochism was that the works were dramatic, not personal expressions of his own sexual taste and experience. It would have been a much more persuasive defense if he had simply pointed out that in these supposedly shocking verses the fairly abstract words *sweet, amorous, pain,* and so on recur continually but in fact nothing happens. Again, Swinburne practically never represents a sexual act as "normal" or "perverse"—as Coventry Patmore does constantly. Sexually passionate and politically radical as these 1866 poems sound at first, they are really more aesthetic than erotic or social. The volume is dedicated to "my friend Edward Burne-Jones," to the painter who was one of Rossetti's friends as well and was the closest friend and early associate of William Morris. Burne-Jones was the epitome of what could be called post pre-Raphaelitism. He might have been thought a "fleshly" artist by some, but he was always attracted to the "spiritual," the ideal (and the sexless; the people in his pictures are often androgynous, impossible to identify by sex). Like him, Swinburne was an artist concerned with fantasy—not fornication.

Swinburne's next volumes, *A Song of Italy* (1867) and *Songs Before Sunrise* (1871), are distinctly political in substance, even though they include some odd personal verses that are sexually revealing. The best-known poem in *Songs Before Sunrise* is "Hertha." It combines the vague political radicalism, the anti-orthodox and antiestablishment strain, with a familiar goddess-worshipping masochism. The whole idea once more is literary, abstract, and intellectual, rather than genuinely sensual. For Swinburne, too, the sex fantasy of the strong maternal woman who threatens a weak man is likely to be combined with other fantasies, political and social, so that physical and ideal, personal and public themes are all merged into one often dazzling realization.

In the late 1860s and early 1870s Algernon Charles Swinburne was widely admired as the most brilliant and promising of England's younger poets. He was also widely feared, even detested, as the precursor of a new paganism, a new sexual looseness and perversity that might soon be expected to bring about the downfall of all moral standards and to undermine all piety.

In person he was charming. Anything but a monster, as his friends declared! He had his soft side: he grieved deeply when a favorite sister died. He also had his sentimental side: his verses about babies are incredibly saccharine. And, certainly, he had his very human weaknesses.

To maintain such vitality, that little body topped by fiery hair must have been amazingly sturdy—and Swinburne prided himself on his physical strength, especially as a swimmer—to withstand what he did to it: the visits to dubious ladies in St. John's Wood who obliged by whipping him heartily; the rounds of drinking that left him inert and badly hung over for days; the periods of frenetic gaiety and self-indulgence followed by periods of dullness and depression.

Perverted or brilliantly daring, monster or charming companion, débauché or suffering hero, he was a meteoric figure.

And he seemed to be endlessly active, endlessly productive. He lived alone but dined out regularly with lion hunters who were not afraid to entertain a fairly infamous celebrity. He published *Erechtheus* and a second series of *Poems and Ballads,* as well as his *Study of Shakespeare.* And he went on drinking. His alcoholic bouts often left him in such a state of chills and fever that he had, once or twice a year, to take himself off to his family home, to his mother, to be nursed back to something like health again. (The question of what Lady Jane Swinburne was really like is intriguing, but she *seems* to have been a remarkably tolerant, loving, and intelligent mother, and not the maternal being —threatening, overwhelming, castrating—of the poet's fantasies.)

In his thirties he was profligate, proud, rebellious, self-indulgent, and, by general if often grudging admission, something of a genius.

Yet we know surprisingly little about him other than these generalizations. Certainly his poems, so passionate and so apparently personal in tone (although they hint at dark doings), actually reveal next to nothing about his private life, his emotional life as in fact he lived it, his sexual life. There is still something mysterious about this man who was regarded as the most libertine of all Victorian writers.

What we do know comes in large part from his letters. For he was an inveterate letter writer. As Cecil Lang's edition of *The Swinburne Letters* shows, he was, when in top form, as much a genius in this kind of writing as he was in poetry, drama, prose fiction, or criticism.

Swinburne's letters to his many friends—to Dante Gabriel and William Rossetti, to Meredith, above all to Monckton Milnes—are full of wit and critical intelligence; sometimes they are bawdy. Many could hardly have been published at the time under his own name, even if he did consistently use dashes in his comic verse (much of it parody) instead of spelling out the "dirty" words: c--t, f---, a---hole, and so on abound in his letters to the closest friends. Sometimes, too, he lapsed into French for the most daring comments. But that was only natural, since he associated sexual daring with his great and inevitable favorite, the Marquis de Sade.

The works of Sade were available only in rare or underground editions, although his reputation was widespread in Victorian England. (Tennyson once shocked Henry James by referring to Sade at a tea party.) But Milnes naturally included them in his library of pornographic volumes and, in 1862, he had been persuaded to lend the eager young poet a copy of *Justine*. Swinburne was determined, at twenty-five, to react to this heady stuff with the sophistication that might be expected of a man who moved in the best literary circles, was intimate with Meredith, published in Dickens's *Once a Week,* and dined at Fryston. He wrote Milnes a long, long letter about how much he had to laugh at the novel, about how boring finally the sexual excesses became through sheer repetition. His reaction appeared, in fact, to be that of many another reader who is bored instead of titillated by "the divine Marquis." But this first critical reaction, which amounts almost to a shrugging off of sadism, is not at all consistent with the way Swinburne reverted to the subject from then on, in letter after letter.

His letters of the late 1860s and the 1870s gradually became quite frank about this fascination with Sade and with sadomasochism. Swinburne never lacked humor, and some of his references to Sade are funny (he wrote that he was as surprised by Mill's approval of his supposedly shocking *Poems and Ballads*— although pleased, for he admired Mill—as he would be to hear of Carlyle's fervent admiration for *Justine*). But, for all his chaffing, and his use of obscene language for the purposes of parody, it becomes clear as one goes through these documents how deeply important to him sadism was. Sadism, that is, in the strict sense of the word: the taking of specifically sexual pleasure in physical pain.

At least one recent critic has leaped from this fact to the assumption that Swinburne was basically and actively homosexual, largely it seems on the premise that anybody who is sexually "perverted" in one way must be "queer" in all other possible ways. (Homosexuality has become so familiar a phenomenon that it appears now to be the normal, the basic, form of so-called sexual deviation, to which others may or may not be added!) Again, the question of Swinburne's homosexual activity is unanswered and probably unanswerable. Some letters might be read as hints of such a tendency. He gloats over tales of school*boys* being flogged until bloody (is he remembering his Eton days and fantasizing about himself as the victim?) ; he refers once or twice to a young boy's having—or losing—great beauty; and in an 1876 letter to Monckton Milnes, now Lord Houghton, he reports with glee the tale of a Bulgarian, one Sadick Bey, who was accused of violating hundreds of "Bulgarian girls *(sic)*," going on to insist that since the very term *bugger* comes from *Bulgarian* they must really have been young boys who were raped.

Still, Swinburne was fascinated by all scandalous forms of sex—by all sex, that is to say, except the normal. He dwelled on lesbianism in his letters as in his poetry and fiction. And we have seen that incest of one kind or another occurs repeatedly in his writing. That theme is almost certainly related to what he regarded as the great love of his life, his love for his own first cousin, Mary Gordon.

They virtually grew up together, and Mary may have seemed more like a sister than a cousin to him. At any rate, their intimacy could never have legally been consummated in marriage. Just how far that intimacy went in their adolescence is not certain; but there are hints in Swinburne's fiction, which repeats obsessively the pattern of love between cousins (which family pressures frustrate), along with the familiar Swinburnean matter of sadomasochistic sexual play: teasings, birchings, whippings that give pain and ecstacy. Some of this might imply that young Mary Gordon enjoyed as much as he did the kind of sexual fun and games that include mastery and subservience, beatings and tears.

Maybe Swinburne dramatized his blighted affection for Mary, as Byron did his love for his half-sister Augusta (both poets were fascinated by incest). But her image and her memory throughout the poet's mature work suggest that his youthful passion for her was genuine, painfully so. There is no more despairing expression anywhere within his work than in the lines he published soon after she married.

That marriage, to a Colonel Disney Leith, occurred in 1865. When the 1866 *Poems and Ballads* appeared, it included a long lament about lost love that, we know today, was addressed to Mary. It begins,

> Before our lives divide for ever...
> . . . . .
> I will say no word that a man might say

> Whose whole life's love goes down in a day;
> For this could never have been; and never,
> Though the gods and the years relent, shall be.

If their union could have been, he continues, she and he would have seemed "Twain halves of a perfect heart, made fast/ Soul to soul while the years fell past." "But now, you are twain, you are cloven apart,/ Flesh of his flesh, but heart of my heart." The poet's further reaction now is interesting psychologically:

> I will go back to the great sweet mother,
> Mother and lover of men, the sea.
> I will go down to her, I and none other,
> Close with her, kiss her and mix her with me.

The speaker is aware that his language implies death by drowning, that his oceanic mother, like Meleager's in *Atalanta,* is a destructive force. Again, death and sexual love are one for Swinburne. The last line here and much that follows it carry a strongly sexual quality, suggesting a love that goes beyond the conventionally acknowledged filial or maternal affections. And it appears significant that this frustrated lover who turns to a mother figure also represents in his prose fiction several mothers who are pointedly shown as sexually attractive.

Even though his letters reveal that during these years Swinburne had many good friends and correspondents, the fact remains that he was essentially alone. His loyal family was in the country; Mary was a wife and soon to be a mother; the whipping women in St. John's Wood were satisfactory only now and then; and Meredith was busy, while Rossetti was too far gone both physically and psychologically to be much help. Unlike Rossetti, he discovered himself incapable of having a settled sexual relationship with—of living with—a mistress.

He discovered that in 1867. That was when he became intimate—but not altogether intimate—with the extraordinary Adah Isaacs Menken.

Adah Isaacs Menken, born in Louisiana, casually married to various men in various places (at least one of the marriages proved to be illegal), burst on the London scene in 1864 with the impact of a bomb. Although she styled herself actress and poet, she was more like a vaudeville or music hall entertainer; the sharp-tongued said that she was also a semi-professional lady of easy virtue. She had been the mistress of Alexandre Dumas *père,* among others, when Swinburne got to know her. On the stage, however, her greatest role was in the extravagant *Mazeppa*: she appeared in flesh-tinted tights—at first glance she seemed to be stark naked—strapped to a horse. Men went wild over her.

And she encouraged them, by her breezy if vulgar vitality as well as by pointing up her buxom beauty. Buxom, in the style favored by mid-Victorian men, she certainly was; and she made a striking figure in her tights. She might be thought a strange intruder into the sphere of the arts, now dominated by the pre-Raphaelite ideal (so far as femine beauty was concerned) of the languorous lady. But she was attracted to artists and writers. She wanted her own poetry to be taken seriously. And the very contrast between her energy, even her coarseness, and the "lilies and languors of virtue" was exciting. Just how fully she represented the "raptures and roses of vice" to Swinburne is in some doubt; but both phrases come from his 1866 "Dolores," and a year later "Dolores" was his name for Adah.

Did she woo him or did he woo her? Whichever way it began, it was soon known that he was the lucky man who had, for the moment, the devotion of this tempestuous creature. That she was actually sharing quarters with Swinburne—she was statuesque, he was tiny; and both could be flamboyant to the point of seeming ridiculous—at once became a joke about which *Punch* and private wits made further jokes. Swinburne was unwise enough to admit that he could not consummate the sexual act with this formidable female; they grappled a bit and decided it was hardly worth the trouble. And this failure to have sexual relations on the part of two who were popularly supposed to be the most lascivious, the most libidinous of public figures—that was the biggest joke yet. It was almost certainly no joke to Swinburne.

The self-advertising Adah Isaacs Menken was forgotten soon; Mary Gordon was gone, if not out of his life, then out of his most intimate life. He wrote. He drank. This was, paradoxically, his most productive decade—from 1868 to 1878—and the time when he very nearly killed himself by his own excesses.

At the end of this period, his second series of *Poems and Ballads* summed up many of Swinburne's personal as well as literary interests. It included a number of translations from the French of Villon and Hugo, and a number of tributes to French writers: Hugo, Baudelaire, Gautier. But it also included a personal note that reverberates in line after line of poem after poem—in, for instance, "A Forsaken Garden":

> the same wind sang and the same waves whitened,
> And or ever the garden's last petals were shed,
> In the lips that had whispered, the eyes that had lightened,
> Love was dead.
> Love was dead.

In Swinburne's life, love was dead.

And the deepest friendship he was to know, the most devoted, was just about to begin.

Swinburne had met Theodore Watts in 1872. (It was later on that Watts had his name hyphenated into Watts-Dunton.) Watts was a solicitor, an avid reader, an admirer of the more advanced poets; he became Swinburne's legal advisor. Not very long afterward, Watts tried to save Dante Gabriel Rossetti from the decline into which he had evidently fallen. Rossetti, determined —or so it might seem—upon his own destruction, was not amenable to guidance. But by 1879 Swinburne was. He was constantly drunk; very possibly he was starving, not for lack of money to buy food but for lack of interest in eating. His mother had again and again come to his rescue; but now he was too weak and lethargic, as he lolled in his London roominghouse, even to write her. Watts-Dunton, as he now styled himself, knew the situation. And, whatever his motives—a desire to be associated with the literary great, an interest in having his name memorialized by literary history, or just plain good-heartedness—he came to the rescue.

He swept Swinburne off to his suburban house, "The Pines," in Putney.

And there he lived, Swinburne the red-headed radical, the scandalous, the obscene and blasphemous, from 1879 until his death a full thirty years later—in the suburbs, in *Putney*!

He did not, however, stop writing or publishing. What he wrote, as a matter of fact, was still capable of irritating and indeed of shocking his contemporaries. In 1880, almost as if it were a sign of his miraculous recovery, he published four volumes: a critical study of Shakespeare, two collections of lyric poems, and a book of poetic parodies.

Many of these works of 1880—and the rest of the decade—were either begun or largely written earlier. Still, Swinburne was now in a healthy enough state of mind and body to see them through the press. Even though his very best writing in verse had been done earlier, his continued activity, especially in literary criticism, was a tribute both to the care of Watts-Dunton and to his own vitality, his own ambition.

Probably the most interesting of the later long poems is *Tristram of Lyonesse*. Here he was deliberately challenging his contemporaries who had treated the same subject.

Inevitably, his version was compared with Matthew Arnold's, the first modern retelling of it in poetry; with Tennyson's, in *The Idylls of the King*; and even with Richard Wagner's opera, which Swinburne knew very well. The differences are revealing.

The subject of these works is, of course, adultery. It was a delicate subject. Matthew Arnold, who was capable of prudery, responded to it more in sorrow than in anger. His shocked reaction to Mill's assertion of the right to regulate one's own private sexual conduct regardless of the marriage laws suggests that, for him, Arthurian lovers may not have come under quite the same strictures as Victorian lovers. At any rate, his beautiful "Tristram and Iseult"—it is his finest long poem—reveals the poet's belief that sexual passion inevitably cools and cannot dominate the lives of men and women without their ultimately being disillusioned, or worse.

Tennyson's passage on Tristram and Isolt in the *Idylls,* near the end of "The Last Tournament," shows how adultery ends in bitterness, in violence, ends with vengeful death. Much more than Arnold's, his attitude is moralistic. But Tennyson came more and more to think that the moral point of his *Idylls,* which began *without* a clear moral point, was that the world is corrupted—certainly by adulterous affairs, probably by sex itself, and possibly by the existence of the body.

Wagner's musical drama is another matter. It celebrates the tragic conclusion to a great sexual passion, but it does not moralize on the event. Very much unlike Arnold and Tennyson, it includes sexual elements that might have shocked them but surely did not shock Swinburne. The foremost of these is the homosexual triangle of King Mark, Melot, and Tristan. Even modern critics and producers have tried to ignore or gloss over that element, but there can be no doubt that it does exist. It exists, and it both enlarges and emphasizes the Wagnerian sense of sexuality as an elemental force that breaks through rules, through mores, even if in doing so it leads to death.

Swinburne's poem is probably closer in spirit to Wagner than to the verse of his fellow English poets. But it has its own special bias. That is a bias against marriage.

In his letters and casual comments, he asserted hostility toward that institution—perhaps not the reasoned opposition to a one-sided contract that we find in Mill or indeed the consideration for women's rights that we find in Meredith, but a dislike of conventional and total sexual commitment. There may be a feeling of personal loss, of frustration, in that hostile attitude. He wrote to congratulate Edmund Gosse on his marrying, and added something about a "jealous afterthought," about his own failure to achieve—with Mary Gordon—what Gosse had. If so, Swinburne made a virtue and a conviction of being frustrated. In his *Tristram*, adultery is accepted and marriage is seen as empty.

Tristram's marriage to the "other Iseult," in this version, is a failure; it is called, in the title of Part IV, a "Maiden Marriage," which means that like Swinburne's sexual relation with Adah Isaacs Menken, it was never consummated. "White-handed Iseult, maid and wife," curses Tristram, her nominal husband, along with his "harlot" and vows that she will avenge herself on both. Her frustration, however, is only a part of the malaise which is general in this poem. It ends with a death that represents escape at last from pain and passion, an escape which the poet seems always to crave.

He lived well into his seventies.

Swinburne continued to write and publish both criticism and poetry up to the end of—and a little bit after—the Victorian age. His prose fiction appeared under his own name only in the twentieth century: *Love's Cross Currents* in 1905 (first published under a pseudonym in 1877) and *Lesbia Brandon* in 1952. (The latter was edited by Randolph Hughes, a waspish but mostly admirable scholar, who pointed out that this inappropriate title was invented by Gosse, rather than the author, in his largely unreliable *Life* of Swinburne.) But, as we have seen, this is fiction of the 1860s and 1870s.

It is as revealing psychologically as it would have been—to his contemporaries—shocking. The late Edmund Wilson believed that Swinburne's narrative prose provided a clearer insight into the Victorian period than any other literary work. It can undoubtedly provide some insight into Swinburne himself, into his sexual interests, and into the underground currents of sexuality in his time. It involves sadism, masochism, incest, some ambiguous elements of homosexuality—in fact, everything except sex within a happy marriage.

The close relation of *Love's Cross Currents* to the other work and the fragmentary and extremely complicated nature of the whole so-called *Lesbia Brandon* manuscript make it impossible to sum up the various plots briefly. (Hughes's commentary on the matter runs to well over two hundred pages.) But one can follow Swinburne's editor in distinguishing certain repeated characters, or types of characters, as well as the constant themes of cruelty and incest.

First, there is the adolescent boy, clearly a projection of Swinburne's own boyhood personality, who is docile when punished and yet, paradoxically, something of a rebel. Another figure is that of the sadistic older man, a kind of punishing master (he can, literally, be a schoolmaster) who may also be a father. Then there is the boy's physically appealing older sister, who can be involved in teasings and spankings as well as flirtatious sex play. If she marries, her husband is dull and unloved. And, perhaps most important, there is the formidable person of the dominating, demanding, psychologically if not physically sadistic woman who is both wife and mother.

There are also a number of cousins—generally they bear the

same relation to each other that Swinburne and Mary Gordon did, as *first* cousins—whose presence reinforces the hints of incest. All in all, with fathers, sons, brothers, sisters, wives, husbands, *and* cousins, the sexual relations and permutations are so complex that the mind boggles.

Although Swinburne published *Love's Cross Currents* pseudonymously in 1877 as *A Year's Letters,* all of this work of fiction was for him essentially a kind of therapy, a working out on paper of his special fantasies. The work is not quite pornographic, but its characters and situations parallel almost perfectly—with much more subtlety and wit—those in a number of popular Victorian pornographic novels: the sadistic schoolmaster, the incestuously attached brother and sister, and the harsh, seducing mother who is herself seduced. In other words, Swinburne's prose may give us more than a sense of his own private sex fantasies. It may also represent an insight into the sexual undercurrents of his age, with the hidden counterpart of, the other side to, a rigid insistence on the primacy of duty, of discipline, and on the sanctity of mother, home, and family.

Algernon Charles Swinburne died of pnemonia in April of 1909. He was one of the last mid-Victorian giants, but he still had a shocking enough reputation so that there was no question of his being buried in Westminster Abbey. Not that he would have wanted it. He did not even want the Anglican burial rites— which, however, in a modified form, his remaining family insisted on having.

Most of his close friends of the earlier years had already gone. Adah Isaacs Menken died soon after their abortive affair, in 1868, leaving her poems to be published posthumously under the unhappy title *Infelicia*—dedicated to Charles Dickens. Rossetti died in 1882. Meredith died in the same year Swinburne did. But Mary Gordon Leith survived.

It seems appropriate that she wrote the first significant memoir of his life. It may even be appropriate, considering how secret the affairs of this apparently open, daring, flamboyant genius were, that hardly anyone guessed until half a century later how much his cousin and biographer had actually meant to him.

In Mary Gordon Leith's book and in those written about

him since, a good deal has been made, quite properly, of his friendships with other writers and his influence upon writers, artists, and men and women in the London cultural circles of his day.

That influence may in some respects have been dubious. In fact, Swinburne may in some instances be very much to blame. But he was as sensitive to moral and artistic influences—to those of Meredith and Rossetti, for example—as others were sensitive to his.

Swinburne's friends and associates included a number who were not particularly drawn to "acting out" so-called sexual deviations—along with a number who were. Among the former was of course Monckton Milnes, Lord Houghton. We know already about his collection of pornographic books, both stories and pictures, and about his wry and perhaps cynical interest in all the possible oddities of sex. He was an apparently happily married man. He was a remarkably successful politician. He was said to have persuaded the Queen to bestow the Poet Laureateship on Tennyson in 1850. He loved the strange, the new, and the adventurous: he ascended in a balloon and he descended into the ocean in an early diving bell. He even agreed with Mill on the importance of women's rights to property and the vote. For Swinburne, he did at least two important things: he introduced him to Sade and he introduced him to Burton.

Richard Burton was himself a lover of the strange and the adventurous. Sixteen years older than Swinburne and twelve years younger than Milnes, he was as unconventional as the one and as sophisticated as the other.

He was certainly one of those men among Swinburne's circle who were fascinated by sexual deviations—for whatever reason, scientific, scholarly, *or* more personal.

The two men met at a stag breakfast given by Milnes in 1861. They appear to have hit it off at once. According to Arthur Symons, Swinburne declared that they had "a curious fancy, an absolute fascination, for each other." They made an odd-looking pair of friends: Swinburne small, wiry, nervous, and the older Burton tall, big-boned, a swaggering, fine figure of a man. According to one anecdote, Burton once came down a stairway

"carrying Swinburne under his arm." There are some indications
that their intimacy went very far indeed. In one of his indiscreet
letters to Milnes, the poet refers to Burton as "my tempter and
favourite audience," adding that he has been "too many for me."
The meaning is ambiguous; it may well be that Burton gratified
his friend's special tastes by standing in for the whipping ladies
and thrashing him more soundly than the younger man had bar-
gained for—all in the spirit of fun, friendship, sexual gratifica-
tion, and perhaps for Burton, of experimentation.

In any case, the two men were close during the 1860s. Swinburne was impressed by the dash and virility of this daring explorer who had, among other things, discovered Lake Tanganyika. Burton, in turn, expressed admiration for Swinburne's
poetry—he was himself a writer as well as translator—especially
for those poems that were most shocking to the general public.
The references to esoteric sexual practices and tastes did not
shock him at all.

But Richard Burton was not likely to be shocked by such
matters. He had seen a good deal of the world. In fact, his curiosity, his virtually shockproof intelligence, had made him, like
Swinburne, a man with a scandalous reputation.

Richard Francis Burton (later Sir Richard), born at Tor-
quay and educated abroad, served as a very young soldier, under
the distinguished Sir Charles Napier, in the British Sind—the
lower Indus valley of what now is Pakistan. When he was twenty-
four, he was commissioned by Napier to investigate the homosexual brothels of Karachi; he had learned to speak Sindi and
therefore seemed the appropriate officer to undertake this delicate matter. Disguised, he visited the houses of boys, took notes,
and wrote for Napier an extensive report. It included such de-
tails as the fact that adolescent boys were generally preferred to
eunuchs for the purposes of sodomy because their scrotums could
be grasped and used "as a kind of bridle." Napier, dismayed,
went about closing down the three notorious local houses of male
prostitution and tried to banish the traditional street transvest-
ites. Burton had done his duty—his superior never appeared to
think that he had done anything more—and what he found in
the process did not particularly startle him.

That report, however, although commissioned and conscientiously produced, was to haunt Burton for the rest of his life.

This was in 1845; Burton had been in India for three years, had mastered several languages, and was already proficient at writing accounts of native life, along with translations. In the next few years, he wrote a series of reports—none so famous or infamous as the one on those Karachi brothels—and, upon his return to England, a number of informative books. These were *Scinde or the Unhappy Valley, Sindh and the Races That Inhabit the Valley of the Indus, Goa and the Blue Mountains,* all published in 1851, and *Falconry in the Valley of the Indus,* published in 1852. There is very little in these works that bears on sexual habits, exotic or otherwise, of the peoples described.

Yet Burton did have a virtually lifelong interest in sexual practices, and his later writing is remarkably candid on the subject.

In 1853 he set out on a journey that was to make him famous, a journey to Mecca. Disguised as a Pathan—that is, an Afghan living in India—he planned to go from Alexandria to the holy city of Islam, forbidden to Christians, Jews, and all other unbelievers, there to discover more than the half-dozen or so Western explorers of that mysterious area had been able to report. He knew that sacrifices would be involved. For one, he might have to be circumcised. He would also have to traverse the desert from Alexandria to Cairo and on to the goal. There were dangers, too. According to strict Moslem law, an infidel found in the area of Mecca would be killed. At best, an Englishman in disguise would be summarily expelled. The dangers, however, were only further incentives to Burton's adventurous spirit.

To his most recent biographer, the whole affair represents a postponement of his search for a wife—he was still unmarried—and a search instead for the "mother city of Islam," which is called "a reaffirmation of his old love of the forbidden: his mother's continuing triumph." The parallel with Swinburne and his evocations of the sexual, dangerous mother is remarkable.

From Alexandria he traveled to Cairo disguised as a dervish and a doctor—a kind of Egyptian medicine man equipped with

nostrums, candied pills, and a "magic" mirror. He called himself
Mirza Abdulla, the "servant of Allah," and was a great success.

He smoked hashish; he administered drugs of a mild sort
and used his powers of hypnotism to enforce his reputation as a
healer; stained with walnut juice and garbed as a pious pilgrim,
he made—for an English-born and partly Oxford-trained young
Westerner—a remarkably effective imposter. He went from Suez
to the Red Sea to Medina. There was a story that at one point
during the journey, at Pilgrimage Pass, he was discovered by a
young Arab urinating, and not crouching as all Arabs did; thus
revealed as a fake, he was said to have killed the curious Moslem.
Later he refused to confirm or deny the story.

After a month at Medina, Burton proceeded to the holy city
itself. He entered the Kaaba, the most sacred place for Moslems,
and found it simply a small windowless room in the middle of
the Great Mosque, practically empty except for a black stone that
every pilgrim kissed and venerated. He always loved disguise and
dangerous adventure, and penetrating to this Holy of Holies was
a great triumph for him. Yet the most valuable part of his pilgrimage, which made for the most interesting part of his written
account, was not the time spent there or even the short time he
remained in Mecca. His observations about both countryside and
customs made fascinating reading. Some of it was too fascinating
altogether for his editor and publisher, who deleted passages
about Arab sexual customs.

Burton observed that the strict separating of the sexes, represented finally by the institution of the harem, tended to strengthen
psychological and physical ties between members of the same sex.
He was inclined to ascribe the homosexuality of the Arab world
to this fact first of all. But most of his reporting and speculations
about that subject, like his account of harem life, remained in
manuscript form and did not appear in his *Pilgrimage to Al-
Medina and Meccah,* published in 1855 and 1856.

While that work was being edited and published, Burton
was still in the Near East, traveling—sometimes again in disguise—and studying languages, customs, places, always taking
notes. He was in Cairo for a time, then in Bombay. It was in
Aden that he learned of his mother's death, in 1854.

That same year he was planning another hazardous journey, this time to the heart of unexplored northeastern Africa, Somaliland. Although he went to the Somali capital, Harar, practically alone, he was assisted in part of the journey by several other British officers, including a Captain John Hanning Speke. One of the officers was killed and both Burton and Speke were wounded by hostile natives. Such an experience might have been thought likely to bring these two men closer together, two who had braved such danger and difficulty and then come back to tell the tale. It did not. Burton's strained relations with Speke, in fact, had a good deal to do with trouble later in Burton's life.

There was no open break yet. In 1856 Speke went again with Burton on an exploratory venture, this time to search for the African sources of the Nile. (In the same year, Burton's *First Footsteps in East Africa* appeared; later Speke apparently thought it did not do justice to his part in the Somali adventure.) They discovered Lake Tanganyika; and, since Burton was leader of the expedition, he considered—as the public came later to agree— that it was his discovery. While Burton lay ill with a fever, however, Speke went on to find Lake Victoria Nyanza. He believed that he deserved credit for this discovery and at least equal credit with Burton for the discovery of Tanganyika. Speke may well have been jealous of Burton's ability, as a writer, to publicize his own exploits. At any rate, by the time the two returned to England in 1859, their relations had become hostile. The Geographical Society, which had commissioned their journey to the upper Nile, honored Speke above Burton, who felt snubbed; and now the rivalry became a matter of public knowledge.

If Burton was indeed intentionally snubbed, it was largely the result of Speke's reviving old rumors that the reports on homosexuality in Karachi and the later comments on homosexual Arab activities came from Burton's more than scientific interest. He hinted broadly that the dashing Burton, still at thirty-eight unmarried, had enjoyed the favors of some Arab boys himself.

Burton's latest biographer, agreeing that the rumors were malicious, thinks that they had some foundation.

Speke was not, anyway, in a position to throw stones. His closest friend, the one most influential in encouraging his vendetta against Burton, was Laurence Oliphant, a rich young man who had been a reporter and diplomat and was about to become known as a prominent practicing homosexual. Oliphant was then twenty-nine. When he eventually married, at forty-two, it was a marriage in name only, like Ruskin's. Still later, he joined a quasi-homosexual brotherhood group in New York state; and when he went back to England he was charged with corrupting the morals of boys and young men. Whatever his motive, possibly just the bitchery of the anti-homosexual homosexual for whom social condemnation and contempt have been internalized (as they have been for the anti-semitic Jew and the "male-chauvinist" woman), Oliphant supported and intensified Speke's resentments.

Speke's attacks on Burton, then, involved challenging the assertion that Lake Victoria Nyanza was not the true single source of the Nile, intimating that Burton was a cheat if not a charlatan, and also accusing Burton of sexual aberration. The final irony is that Speke himself, who loved no woman except his mother, and whose best friend remained the dubious Oliphant, was at least as vulnerable to such an imputation as his enemy was.

In 1861 all of these rumors and rivalries, accusations and innuendoes, were still in peoples' minds. They were also, almost certainly, rankling in the mind of Richard Burton.

His mother had been dead for seven years. His reputation was tarnished, for all his daring forays into lands, languages, and customs strange to most Englishmen—in part, rather, *because* of those forays. He was forty. Then, in the year he published his book on Utah—concerned with polygamy but no more esoteric sexual customs—and the year when he was to meet Swinburne, Richard Burton did the most surprising thing of all. He got married.

Isabel Arundell was a romantic girl of nineteen when she first saw him in Boulogne, eleven years before their marriage. She had been told by a gypsy that she would marry a man named Burton, and that she would meet him across the sea from England. It all seemed perfect. She came from one of the best old English Catholic (Roman Catholic) families. On the continent, she had the right to call herself Countess Isabel of Arundell (because of the title "Count of the Holy Roman Empire" granted to an ancestor). But she was a nervous as well as a proud young woman. And she was overwhelmed by her first sight of the strangely handsome, dark and muscular man with the great penetrating eyes, as he strode along the ramparts of Boulogne. Still, matters were to be less than easy. She soon learned that he had had various love affairs and that he was now carrying on a flirtation with her own cousin Louisa. Not these facts, not the most terrible fact of all (which she gleaned from his books) —that he was non-Catholic, non-Christian, and by implication anti-religious—nothing was enough to change her conviction that he was the man destined for her. If she was not to be his mate, she wrote after meeting him, she would enter a convent.

She was by no means a simpering pretty little thing, in spite of her blonde and pleasingly plump looks. She felt contempt for the fashionable marriage-market aspect of social life that haunted every debutante; she was determined to avoid being married off to a dull and proper person at any cost (the convent might be the cost). But she *was* genuinely pious. And that was only one reason, perhaps the most startling one, that her marriage to Burton seemed a mismatch.

Mismatch or not, she was determined upon it.

In 1856, at Ascot, she encountered the gypsy woman who had prophesied the marriage. The woman, Hagar, asked if her name was Burton yet, and, when Isabel replied vehemently that it was not but that she wished it were, Hagar said she now had not long to wait. A few months later, she and Burton were engaged.

It was in August of that year that they met again in London, in the Botanical Gardens; Burton was walking with his old flame, Isabel's cousin Louisa (now married), who reintroduced them. In the past few years, Isabel had been tempted several times to try on her own to renew the acquaintance with this man of her dreams and fantasies, but she had decided it would be unwise. Now, almost miraculously, what she had most hoped for was actually happening.

She told him about the gypsy's prediction, about having fallen in love with him some six years earlier, about her willingness, her eagerness, to follow him anywhere. He was angling for the position of consul at Damascus; she would have consented to go into the Bush with him. She was sincere and courageous (she had already written to Florence Nightingale asking, in vain, to be accepted as a nurse in the Crimea). She was also a self-effacing hero-worshipper. If she could only have been a man as she wished, she wrote, she would want to be Richard Burton; a woman, she was intent on being Richard Burton's wife. Some of Burton's friends later hinted that Isabel trapped him into an engagement and ultimately a marriage. If so, he had no objections at the time to being trapped. He enjoyed explaining things to her, explaining Disraeli's novel *Tancred*, the Near East, and the African and Arab worlds he knew, how explorers explored and how writers wrote. He enjoyed spending time with this pretty young woman who was in awe of him, who seemed irresistibly drawn to him by destiny (Burton himself felt some superstition about the prophecy), who was not in the least coy when he proposed but answered yes with passionate intensity as soon as she could catch her breath.

They were engaged in 1856. He left almost at once for Africa, to search for the sources of the Nile.

It was to Isabel, then, as well as the Geographical Society and an English society half-admiring and half-disapproving, that Burton returned in 1859. Although her family, too, seemed rather dubious—her mother was adamant in opposing the marriage—the wedding took place less than two years after that return. It was a Catholic ceremony. Her father, brothers, and sisters finally approved the match, but neither her mother nor his possessive sister did: to the one, he was an infidel and possibly something much worse; to the other, she was a bigot and a fool. No relative was at the wedding.

If relatives failed to rally round, powerful friends did not. Monckton Milnes gave a party to celebrate the event, a party that included Lord Palmerston, then the prime minister, along with the dowager Lady Russell and a dazzling list of political, social, and artistic luminaries.

Isabel had ambitions for her husband, to make him powerful in his political position, respectable in his financial position, and, above all, right in his religious position—that is, a Roman Catholic. She did not realize how much the intimacy with Monckton Milnes, which promised well for the first two ambitions, might undermine her hopes for the third. The fact is that Milnes, the giver of that gala wedding party—and of the party later that year at which Burton met Swinburne—had also, a year and a half earlier, introduced Burton to the notorious sadist and masochist, Fred Hankey. Burton and Hankey remained good friends until the latter died. Swinburne, to whom the Burtons were introduced by Milnes quite soon after their marriage, had something of the same fascination for him that the effeminate Hankey did. Isabel made no comment, but it was all very curious.

Burton and his wife had seven months together before he set out for Fernando Po, an island off West Africa, where he had been appointed consul. He forbade Isabel to go with him.

From then on, Burton remained in the consular service; and for a good part of the time—while he was British consul in Santos (Brazil), Damascus (at last), and Trieste—he was living alone, without his still faithful and adoring wife.

In 1863 he published *Wanderings in West Africa* and *Abeokuta and the Cameroons*; in 1864, *A Mission to Gelele, King of Dahomé*; in 1865, *Wit and Wisdom from West Africa*; in 1869, *The Highlands of Brazil*; in 1870, *Letters from the Battlefields of Paraguay*; in 1872, *Unexplored Syria* and *Zanzibar*; in 1875, *Ultima Thule*; in 1876, *Etruscan Bologna*; in 1877, *Sind Revisited*; in 1879, *The Land of Midian*; in 1883, *To the Gold Coast for Gold*. He devoted himself not to marriage but to diplomacy and to writing.

It was not, however, his original writing so much as his translations that made an impact on the reading public and made Burton famous—and infamous. Or, rather, it was his series of translations, along with his frank notes on sexual customs that went along with those translations. The notes were sometimes very frank indeed, and lacking in the partly moralizing, partly hypocritical additions that the mid-Victorian reader even of pornography might well expect.

Actually, the *Kama Sutra,* the *Arabian Nights,* and *The*

Perfumed Garden, all of which Burton translated, are much more concerned with heterosexual than with homosexual love. This is true even though Isabel, who destroyed Burton's *Perfumed Garden* after his death, implied that the "vice" of which she feared he might still be accused was its main subject.

The *Kama Sutra* is a classic of India, an ancient compilation of advice on various aspects of life, including but not especially emphasizing the sexual. Like the *Perfumed Garden,* which is in effect a manual on sex and marriage, it touches only casually on such matters as oral techniques for homosexuals. Yet Burton was careful to publish all such works (with financial backing from Monckton Milnes) under the imprint of the "Kama Shastra Society of London and Benares." Supposedly they were published in India; in fact, they were printed and distributed in England. But for three centuries, books published in England that could be considered seditious or pornographic had been advertised on their title pages as coming from Paris, Leyden, or some other foreign place. Evidently Burton thought his translations might be regarded as pornographic by prudish readers—and by the law.

Burton's best-known translation, the *Thousand Nights and a Night,* was first published in the same way between 1882 and 1888. In his other, shorter, works of translation, Burton was careful to use only transliterated Arabic words for sexual organs and sexual acts. In the so-called *Arabian Nights,* he decided to use English. He also decided to defend himself and the stories, in advance, against moral attack.

His Introduction to these volumes of tales argues that they contain nothing coarser than what can be found in Shakespeare, Sterne, and Swift. Some passages may startle the English reader because what is accepted in one time and place appears scandalous in another; but, he insists, the stories have no "subtle corruption," no "covert licentiousness"; they are open and healthy-minded.

> Here we have nothing of that immodest modern modesty which sees covert implication where nothing is implied, and "improper" allusion when propriety is not outraged; nor do we meet with the nineteenth century refinement; innocence of the word but not of the thought; morality of the tongue not of the heart, and the sincere homage paid to virtue in guise of perfect hypocrisy.

The *Arabian Nights* stories do, of course, include a good deal that is explicitly sexual. The vast majority of them, however, depend for their interest on the element of adventure rather than any particular dwelling on sexual acts or attributes. In a sense Burton's introduction is right in commenting that many nineteenth-century stories are much more preoccupied with sex than these tales.

Again, the overwhelming majority of stories that involve sex are entirely concerned with heterosexual relations, not with the sin of which Burton himself was suspected. Still, homosexuality does appear; and when it does, the very harshest attitude taken is simply that of disapproval on the part of one character or another.

Burton knew that this might be the most shocking aspect of his translation: his inclusion of stories that revealed not only familiarity with, but a degree of tolerance for, homosexual practices. Tolerance and, now and then, sympathy. One of the tales most sympathetic toward homosexual love, specifically toward pederasty, is that of "Wazir of Al-Yaman and His Young Brother." It involves a triangle of sorts: a vizier or minister of state, his "young brother of singular beauty," and an old man "of dignified and reverend aspect, chaste and religious," who is made the young boy's tutor and lives next door to the vizier's house. The old man falls in love with the boy and persuades him—without the slightest difficulty—to come next door while the older brother is asleep. There, the old man and the beautiful boy drink and feast on the moonlit terrace. But the vizier awakens, hears them, and climbing to his parapet, sees them. Aware of his presence, the old man improvises these verses:

> He made me drain his wine of honey lips,
> Touching with cheeks which rose and myrtle smother.
> Then nighted in embrace, cheek to my cheek,
> A loveling midst mankind without another.
> When the full moon arose and on us shone
> Pray she traduce us not to the big brother.

The vizier proves his delicacy, saying "By Allah, I will not betray you!" The story ends, "And he went away and left them to their diversions." There is in Petronius an anecdote that strikingly parallels this tale—and yet is very different. In Petronius the old tutor seduces the young boy with gifts: the man is goatish (his motive is lust), the beautiful boy is calculating (until sexually aroused, when he wants to be sodomized again and again), and the whole story amounts to a bawdy joke. The contrast between that joke and the delicate tale Burton translated, in which love and consideration move the characters, underlines Burton's point about the *Arabian Nights,* that they are not pornographic even when they are frankly sexual.

Still, we can wonder what Isabel Burton thought of the "Wazir of Al-Yaman and His Young Brother."

Burton's concern not only to defend the tales against charges of lewdness but also to defend his work as one of serious scholarship is made quite clear in the "Terminal Essay" to the translation. This is actually a series of essays on various aspects of the *Arabian Nights* and the culture from which the collection came. Near the end of it, in a brief comment on "Pornography," he introduces that most delicate feature, about which he proceeds to discourse at length.

> But I repeat there is another element in The Nights and that is one of absolute obscenity utterly repugnant to English readers, even the least prudish. It is chiefly connected with what our neighbors call *Le vice contre nature*— as if anything can be contrary to nature which includes all things.

The first sentence sounds almost priggishly acquiescent to general opinion, with the innocent translator protesting too much. But the second sentence subtly mocks the first. We realize that it does this when we read the note appended to it, in which Burton cites a fictional dying fisherman who, on his deathbed, cries to his confessor,

> Oh! Oh! your reverence, to amuse myself with boys was natural to me as for a man to eat and drink; yet you asked me if I sinned against nature!

John Stuart Mill had already made the point that, strictly speaking, nothing can be contrary to nature, in the first of his posthumously-published *Three Essays on Religion* (1874). Burton was the first to declare boldly that the usual delicate phrase for homosexual relations, "unnatural acts," was meaningless.

What follows is the lengthy essay on "Pederasty." Significantly, it is not entitled "Homosexuality": pederasty in the true
sense, love of young boys, is his main subject. That, of course, is
appropriate because this version of homosexuality is virtually the
only one that appears in the *Arabian Nights*, the one version
that might possibly be accepted in the medieval Arabic world, as
in ancient Greece and modern North Africa. A comparative
anthropologist might be amused to observe that the only form of
homosexual behavior tolerated in those times and places is the
only kind legally condemned in much of the Western world today. As to what distinction the translator and editor of the *Arabian Nights* would make between the relation of man with boy
on the one hand and, on the other, the relation of man with
man, we have no way of knowing for certain; but there is no
doubt that some of his acquaintances were men sexually interested in other men.

The essay on pederasty was to become the most controversial
part of the whole work. But, evidently, Burton meant it to be a
scholarly account and not a defense of particular sexual practices—or, and that was the problem, a condemnation.

It begins with a reference to that early experience with the
male brothels of Karachi. Burton suggests that his interest in the
subject began then; he goes on to outline a theory about pederasty that attributes it to geography and climate. This theory de-
fines a "Sotadic Zone" that includes the southern parts of France,
Portugal, Spain, Italy, and Greece, along with the northern
coastal region of Africa from Morocco to Egypt. The pederasty of
ancient Greece is, inevitably, considered—and considered in its
idealized version as well as its purely physical expressions.

Early in the essay, Burton gives evidence of profoundly
ambivalent feelings about his subject. Sometimes his references to
sodomy are couched in the conventional language that includes
such phrases as "abominable practice"; sometimes he implies (if
he does not actually state) a certain sympathy, even admiration,
for the male lovers of boys who were and are granted a right to
their sentiments in various cultures.

Quite possibly the most shocking thing in this whole treatment of the homosexual passion was Burton's comment that it
was not limited to the East but that it flourished, in the middle

of the nineteenth century, in all the European capitals—including Paris and London. Again, for the "proper" reading public to be told in cold print what they already very well knew was the greatest outrage there could be.

But the reference to modern capitals was incidental. Burton was much more interested in the variety of sexual practices that came under his heading—sometimes only very loosely—and that provided interesting anthropological evidence as to where, why, and how homosexuality flourished in his "Sotadic" areas. He found instances of institutionalized sodomy—almost always pederastic—not only around the Mediterranean but also among American and Alaskan Indians, and in Peru and Brazil.

Finally, he insisted that the *Arabian Nights* had no more offensive matter than a great many other familiar classics; and he used the last paragraph of his essay on pederasty to launch a counterattack on the relatively few critics who had attacked his translation on moral grounds (the vast majority, perhaps to his surprise, had praised it) :

> In an age saturated with cant and hypocrisy, here and there a venal pen will mourn over the "pornography" of The Nights, dwell upon the "ethics of dirt" and the "garbage of the brothel"; and will lament the "wanton dissemination (!) of ancient and filthy fiction." This self-constituted *censor morum* reads Aristophanes and Plato, Horace and Virgil, perhaps even Martial and Petronius, because "veiled in the decent obscurity of a learned language"; he allows men Latinè loqui; but is scandalized at stumbling-blocks much less important in plain English.

Why not, he concludes, bowdlerize Boccaccio, Chaucer, Shakespeare, Rabelais, Sterne, Swift, and the Old Testament? Educated largely in France, he may not have been aware that every one of these *had* in fact been bowdlerized!

There remains, finally, something ambiguous not only about this essay but also about the other notes and comments in which Burton touches upon homosexuality.

Still, the overall effect of Burton's work, including his commentary, was to suggest that such variant forms of sexual behavior as pederasty (and lesbianism, which he also touches on) were

neither "unnatural" nor, considering mankind as a whole, especially rare. In 1885, the year when his remarks on the subject
first appeared, Parliament enacted a law that, for the first time,
made private homosexual acts between males punishable by imprisonment. The law applied only to men because Queen Victoria could not believe such things could ever happen among
women. (Victoria, a devoted wife and grief-stricken widow, the
mother of nine children, knew about sex; but her knowledge was
distinctly circumscribed.) Of the prominent Victorian men affected, Simeon Solomon was prosecuted under the old law for
public lewdness, but Oscar Wilde's case came under the new law,
only ten years after its passage. Burton's 1885 essay can be read as
a cool-headed response to public and parliamentary hypocrisy.

Burton's life in the 1880s was quieter than before. His intimates, to whom the marriage with Isabel had always seemed
strange (again, he was away from her more than he was with
her), were surprised to see her start to take over his life; she even
baptized him when he was desperately ill. She was with him at
his deathbed—in Trieste, where he had served as consul for almost twenty years.

After his death, Isabel offended Burton's friends in several
ways. She burned his full translation, never published, of *The
Perfumed Garden,* defending herself by suggesting that it dealt
with sexual vice (presumably homosexuality, for she was even
more haunted by that threat ᵗo his reputation than he had
been). And she had him buried in a Catholic ceremony. An outraged Swinburne wrote, in his elegy for his friend, "Priests and
the soulless serfs of priests." It was more diatribe against Isabel
than eulogy for Richard.

Burton's reputation was not much helped by the admirers
who wrote of him after he died. Swinburne fulminated. Isabel, in
her huge and adulatory account, practically invented a new personality after her own image—not only a deeply loving husband
but a man who was at heart religious. The biography is almost
idolatrous. Worst of all, her attempts to refute the rumors of his
sexual deviation could only fan the flames of those rumors.

Fawn Brodie, Burton's latest biographer, concludes that he
probably did experiment with homosexuality in his youth—as he

experimented with a number of special indulgences. He was always intrigued by the forbidden. True, he had love affairs with
several women, even had some mistresses, and attempted several
seductions; but, for a Burton, that would hardly rule out the possibilities of boys, perhaps even men. (He also drank heavily, in
alcoholic bouts with Milnes and Swinburne, but that hardly
ruled out his experimenting with hashish.) He was fascinated,
too, by sadism and by masochism, as both his friendship with
Swinburne in London and his intimacy with the notorious Fred
Hankey in Paris suggest. Even after his marriage he appears to
have had some homosexual experiences—if we can interpret correctly what he wrote to Milnes and Swinburne. And they may
well have involved some mild sadism.

But Burton's private life, his sexual life, is still as mysterious
and as tantalizing to the biographer as Swinburne's. Again, what
we have that can be called definite is what he wrote on sex.

This is certainly not the work of literary genius. The verse
translation in the story of the old man and the beautiful boy
shows that he was not much of a poet. His prose, too, is uneven.
And his main claim, that is, to be a serious scholar, has been
disputed.

Even his reputation as a daring explorer has suffered. Almost a hundred years after his death, Burton is sometimes represented as more a publicist than an adventurer, more a *poseur*
than a diplomat. He was a complex man, capable of some dissembling; but these judgments are certainly unfair.

The point is that Burton's interest for us need not depend
upon his personal sexual daring or upon any consistently reliable
scholarship, need not depend in fact upon his being one of the
great explorers. The point is that he was curious enough, bold
enough, and at least sometimes candid enough, to speak and
write of human behavior, including sexual behavior, without
hypocrisy—and to attack the hypocrisy of the world around him.

Practically every public man in this age was obliged now and
then to trim, to be discreet instead of saying or writing what he
really thought. This was true of Burton. Yet he was more nearly
consistent and more honorable in what he said and wrote than

almost any one of his contemporaries who had reason to be nervous about their reputations.

John Stuart Mill, for example, actuated no doubt by the best of reasons—that is, by the wise politician's concern for the immediate possible good and not the distant impossible ideal—was less than candid in his public exposition of women's sexual and social rights.

Algernon Swinburne, supposedly so daring, trimmed *his* sails when there was real danger. He lacked Burton's courage, and he certainly lacked Mill's tactical justification when—after all his poetic boldness and bluster—he deserted the man he had once encouraged and admired, the man he had quite possibly seduced: the clever, touching, tragic Simeon Solomon.

Swinburne had the greatest influence of any person on the life of this strange and sensitive man. Solomon, a mystical painter and would-be poet who was deeply attracted to religious rites and symbols, especially the Catholic, might appear to be as unlike the virile, bold, and candidly skeptical Richard Burton as possible. Yet the almost feminine artist and the aggressively male explorer had something in common that always fascinated Swinburne: both were exotics.

Solomon, of a Jewish family, had Mediterranean features and coloring, while Burton looked like a gypsy; both could be considered somehow not "really English." Furthermore, both were fascinated by the forbidden subject of sexual deviation.

Unfortunately, the facts of Solomon's life are shadowy. He summed them up himself in

A History of Simeon Solomon
From his cradle to his grave

As an infant he was very fractious. He developed a tendency toward designing. He had a horrid temper. He was pampered. He illustrated the Bible before he was sixteen.

He was hated by all of his family before he was eighteen. He was eighteen at the time he was sent to Paris. His behavior there was so disgraceful that his family—The Nathans, Solomons, Moses, Cohens, *etc.*, et hoc genus homo—would have nothing to do with him. He returned to London to pursue his disgraceful course of Art, wherein he displayed such marvelously exquisite effects of coleography that the world wondered. He then turned his headlong course into another channel—that of illustrating books for youths. His "Vision of Love Revealed in Sleep" is too well known. After the publication of this his family repudiated him forever.

His appearance is as follows:

Very slender, dark, a scar on one or two eyebrows, a slouching way with him, a certain nose, one under lip.

That is
S. S.

Of course, this ironic self-portrait was written long before the subject went to his grave, but the tone of it—a comic pretense that the world knew his early art or that his book-length poem was known to anyone, along with a wry acknowledgment of the painful fact that his family had disowned him—foreshadows the tragicomic quality of Solomon's later life.

Born in 1840 or thereabout of a rich London mercantile family—his father, a hat manufacturer, was the first Jew to be given the freedom of London—he entered the Royal Academy School at fifteen and was so precocious that he exhibited his first painting when he was eighteen. His earliest pictures were inspired by Biblical stories and characters and displayed a skill in drawing and in color that impressed several critics, including Thackeray, who especially praised *The Finding of Moses* in his 1860 *Roundabout Papers*. He gradually came under the influence of pre-Raphaelitism, however, and his work began to resemble first Rossetti's, then Burne-Jones's. His subject matter, that is, became both more Catholic and more Catholic. His drawing tended more and more to the stylized, the idealized. His coloring grew more brilliant. Most striking of all, he was soon producing versions of the androgynous figure one finds so often in both Rossetti and Burne-Jones, the figure whose sex is sometimes indeterminate. But where the better-known pre-Raphaelites were inclined to draw strong-limbed, long-necked, and Amazonian women with great chins and heavy brows, young Solomon drew and painted dreamy men with delicate features and feminine grace.

By the late 1860s, and Solomon's late twenties, his brief
Parisian training and much of his academic manner, too, had
been forgotten. He could now generally be regarded as a pre-
Raphaelite artist. A painting dated 1870, *The Mystery of Faith*
(now in the Lady Lever Gallery at Port Sunlight), illustrates his
style. It shows a young priest holding a monstrance—the elaborate vessel in which the Host is displayed for adoration—and
gazing at it solemnly. The picture is an odd, pre-Raphaelite combination of ascetic and aesthetic. The priest's lean, delicate young
face is dominated by his great, luminous eyes. (Whether or not
Solomon intended the resemblance, he looks something like a
young John Henry Newman.) The effect is slightly but dis-
turbingly epicene. His cope and chasuble are elaborately deco-
rated and gorgeously colored, as is the golden monstrance and
the altar behind. The richness and decoration are accurate, but
they also remind one of the lush allover patterns one finds every-
where in Morris and Rossetti. The total effect of this painting is
an exaggeration, however, of pre-Raphaelite voluptuous mysticism: the richness, the almost feminine priest, the extremely
phallic monstrance seem to combine religious imagery with something mysteriously sensual—and distinctly sexual.

Solomon's own brief account of his life gives no indication as
to why his family and close relatives—the Solomons, Nathans,
Moseses, and Cohens—repudiated him. It may have had something to do with a shift of interest suggested by his change in
subject matter—from such Old Testament stories as *The Finding
of Moses* to such distinctly Christian and Catholic scenes as that
in the *Mystery of Faith*. He may have been regarded as an apos-
tate, as one who deserted his religious heritage. (According to
one version, Solomon died as a Roman Catholic.)

Another possibility is that his wildness led him even as a
young man into some dubious associations and some scrapes involving his always special sexual tastes.

His early artist friends, Henry Holiday, Marcus Stone, and
Albert Moore (later to be a celebrated painter), were not especially scandalous figures. But Solomon hints at a dissolute young
life—and he may or may not be trying to make a glamorous
figure of himself. In any event, of his activities, his relations

with his family, his family itself, we know little. There is one hint, only, that his sister Rebecca, also talented as an artist, had lesbian tendencies. If this is so, and if we had some documents about the background of these two, the whole story of the Solomon family might be very interesting.

In 1870 he was just about thirty years old. He was no longer a precocious youth, and he was not yet an established artist. Associated in the journalistic mind with the once despised and now dominant "school" of the pre-Raphaelites—and by now there was no such thing as a school to which that term could apply—he appeared to be at a turning point in his life.

He was writing poetry that year: the book-length *Vision of Love Revealed in Sleep,* which he arranged to have published privately. (Not because he was afraid, like Burton, that his work would be found pornographic, but because no commercial publisher was interested.)

Rossetti's essay "Hand and Soul," first published in the 1850 pre-Raphaelite journal *The Germ,* may have suggested the aesthetic ideas of this visionary poem, as William Fredeman suggests. But the major influence on Solomon's literary style was not Rossetti. There is some sort of poetic justice in the fact that Swinburne commented on the weakness of the poem, on its lack of that coherence which is

> requisite to keep symbolic or allegoric art from absolute dissolution and collapse, that unity of outline and connection of purpose, that graduation of correlative parts and significance or corresponsive details, without which the whole aerial and tremulous fabric of symbolism must decompose into mere confusion and fruitless chaos.

The poetic justice, the irony, of this comment is that it applies perfectly to most of the critic's own verse. If any poet was likely to have his "aerial and tremulous fabric" of verse "decompose into mere confusion and fruitless chaos," it was Swinburne.

Solomon's poem is, in its allegorical and very vague outlines as well as its alliterative style, derivative from Swinburne—and not the best of Swinburne—even though the final vision of love attempts an erotic version of Dante with more than a touch of Coventry Patmore. Like Swinburne (and the later Rossetti)

Solomon, the poet, gave his Eros a religious aura but associated it, too, with swooning, pain, and death.

Solomon wrote the *Vision of Love* before meeting his master and critic, just as he developed a pre-Raphaelite manner in painting before meeting the pre-Raphaelites. He was evidently susceptible to being swayed by powerful men and movements. He was even more susceptible to powerful personalities in correspondence and in private intercourse, as his few extant letters show.

It was in 1870 that they met; for three years they were friends and frequent correspondents. Clearly, Swinburne was flattered by the frank adulation of the painter, and Solomon was flattered by the interest of so brilliant a poet—especially since he had aspirations to poetic achievement himself. In 1871 he wrote to ask if Swinburne would review his poem in an article that might also comment on his pictures. It was, as Solomon put it, a supplication. And of course Swinburne agreed: "Simeon Solomon: Notes on His *Vision of Love,* and Other Studies" appeared in the *Dark Blue* that July. As we just saw, it was not completely favorable.

There had been speculation about Swinburne's specific influence upon the younger man's sex life as well as his artistic career—speculation about his having seduced Solomon either quite literally or by introducing him to evenings that included not only sado-masochistic diversions but specifically homosexual ones. Whatever the truth, there can be no doubt that Swinburne's dissipations at this period did encourage emulation; Solomon may not have been a sober innocent before their meeting, but soon afterward he began his course of heavy indulgence in drinking, drugs, and underground adventures that resulted in his criminal associations and his troubles with the law.

Rossetti admired him; Burne-Jones called him "the greatest artist of us all"; Thackeray and Pater praised him highly; Swinburne, his clearest-headed critic, became his closest friend. Virtually all of them were willing to ignore him or condemn him when, in 1873, poor Solomon got into serious trouble that might have threatened the reputations of his friends.

The most nearly explicit account of what happened is a

legal document, a jury's indictment that is dated February, 1873, and headed—with no humor intended—*Middlesex*.

> The Jurors for Our Lady the Queen upon their oath present That *George Roberts* and *Simeon Solomon* on the eleventh day of February in the year of our Lord one thousand eight hundred and seventy three unlawfully and wickedly did attempt and endeavour to commit a certain felony, that is to say that the said George Roberts and Simeon Solomon on the day and year aforesaid unlawfully and wickedly did attempt and endeavour feloniously and wickedly and against the order of nature to commit and perpetuate with each other that detestable and abominable crime of Buggery against the Peace of Our Lady the Queen her Crown and Dignity.

> *Second Court* And the Jurors aforesaid do further present that the said George Roberts and Simeon Solomon on the same day and in the year aforesaid in a certain urinal frequented and resorted to by many of the liege subjects of Our Lady the Queen for a necessary purpose and in a certain and open place called Stratford Place Mews situated in the Parish of Saint Marylebone in the County of Middlesex, and near and adjacent to a certain Highway and Footpath there situated and in the sight and view of many of the liege subjects of Our Lady the Queen then and there being, and then and there repassing did resort together for the purpose of committing with each other diverse lewd and unnatural practices and did then and there commit and perpetuate with each other diverse such practices as aforesaid. And that he the said George Roberts did and there in such open and public place as aforesaid and within the sight and view of such persons as aforesaid unlawfully and wickedly expose his private members naked and uncovered for a long space of time to wit for the space of fifteen minutes. And that the said Simeon Solomon did then and there in such open and public place as aforesaid unlawfully and wickedly expose his private members for a long space of time to wit fifteen minutes. To the great damage and common nuisance of all the liege subjects of Our Lady the Queen then and there being and then and there passing and repassing And Against the Peace of Our Lady the Queen and Crown and Dignity.

The picture of those liege subjects passing and repassing is a fascinating one: it suggests a degree of curiosity—otherwise, why repassing?—that may have implied an uncomfortable amount of interest, that may have triggered, out of nervousness and guilt, a desire to betray whatever indiscretion was occurring to the proper authorities.

But what was occurring?

The reference to "Buggery" would indicate anal intercourse —except that all such terms in the nineteenth century, including "sodomy" and "pederasty," were so loosely used as to make them nearly meaningless. It is, of course, possible, that anal intercourse was attempted. It seems more likely that there was some oral contact. It also seems likely that, if two men were exposing themselves in an inviting way for anything like fifteen minutes—even allowing for a great deal of exaggeration in the legal document— this urinal was a place where these things regularly happened. (Stratford Place Mews was, and is, a cul-de-sac off Oxford Street and thus in the heart of London's busiest area.) Either that, or we must assume that such things could occur in any London urinal—and that, too, might have been the case.

Solomon's crime, this document makes clear, was regarded largely as a sin—he behaved both "unlawfully and wickedly"— for on sexual points the law made no distinction between secular rules and the morality associated with religion. Furthermore, the jurors' language reveals a more than legal or merely moral degree of opprobrium, a real fear and horror: the act of homosexual intercourse is "detestable and abominable," "lewd," and, inevitably, "unnatural."

Some Victorian scandals could be hushed up or at least muffled. Unfortunately, this one became public knowledge.

And most of the public who knew of it felt obliged to express the same horror that the jury either felt or, in effect, said they felt. Divorce and adultery were bad enough; sodomy was still far beyond the pale.

The year 1873, approximately the middle point in his life, was also for Solomon the turning point. The man who had been so praised by the pre-Raphaelites—he was briefly an assistant to Millais—who had visited Oxford as Walter Pater's guest, to paint his portrait, who had been entertained at Eton by the great classical scholar, Oscar Browning, who had been, above all, one of

Swinburne's intimates, was dropped now by almost all of them.

Almost, but not quite all. Some friends rallied to his support and had him taken into a private asylum—to rest and to recover from his chronic drunkenness, which was almost certainly responsible for his rash public behavior and his downfall. But the pre-Raphaelite circle did not distinguish itself for generosity or even common humanity. And of all who ignored or turned against Solomon, Swinburne was the one who behaved most badly.

He may have believed that he had the most to lose from being associated with the subject of such a scandal (if so, he was right) ; but his response was worse than cowardly. He spoke piously of Solomon as "a thing unmentionable alike by men and women, as equally abhorrent to either—nay, to the very beasts." This from the author of "Anactoria," the dévoté of Sade, the notorious masochist and débauché!

Solomon's later life is obscure. Supposedly, he sold matches on the street for awhile and then became a sidewalk chalk artist, this painter who had exhibited at the Royal Academy when he was eighteen. ("Supposedly" because at least one scholar doubts the story.) His street life as well as his sexual interests led to associations with boys and men who were pickpockets, thieves, and sometimes blackmailers. At one point, he was involved in an attempt to steal gold leaf from the studio of his former friend, Burne-Jones; he escaped a prison sentence only because of his having once been a gentleman and an artist.

There is a touching but perhaps apocryphal story about these years, according to which Oscar Browning saw Solomon drawing in chalk on a London pavement and leaped out of his carriage to greet and embrace him. Solomon, the story continues, was glad to see his old friend but, on being pressed, declared that he was doing well and needed no assistance. This and other such accounts of his later years have been challenged because there are Solomon drawings and paintings dated in the 1880s that he apparently sold—suggesting he was hardly reduced to the role of sidewalk artist.

At the same time, his habits—which certainly included heavy drinking, almost certainly included some drug-taking, and probably included paying for the sexual favors of boys and young men—may have forced him from time to time to eke out a temporary living in whatever way he could. Whether he was literally reduced to chalk and pavement we cannot be sure; it seems fairly likely, however, that even with what help he had from friends and possibly from relatives in these dark years, he had to use whatever dodges he could to get along. One resort was selling letters written to him by the great and famous. When Swinburne discovered that Solomon had sold some of *his* letters —some that were indiscreet, if not obscene—he was furious. His anger reinforced his nervousness about any association with the former friend and probably justified in his own mind his rejection of Solomon.

It reads as a poignant story, as a tragedy. Yet Simeon Solomon had no intention of being a tragic victim.

All the evidence shows that he refused to be pitied or to pity himself. Robert Ross—like Browning, and very much unlike the frightened Swinburne, a loyal friend—wrote about the Solomon of this period:

> It is a consolation to think that he enjoyed himself in his sordid way. When I had the pleasure of seeing him last, so lately as 1893, he was extremely cheerful and not aggressively alcoholic. Unlike most spoilt wastrels with the artistic temperament, he seemed to have no grievances, and had no bitter stories or complaints about former friends, no scandalous tales about contemporaries who had remained reputable; no indignant feeling towards those who assisted him. This was an amiable, inartistic trait in his character, though it may be a trifle negative; and for a positive virtue, as I say, he enjoyed his drink, his overpowering dirt, and his vicious life. He was full of delightful and racy stories about poets and painters, policemen and prisons, of which he had wide experience.

Whatever Ross meant by Solomon's "sordid way," it seems clear what the "vicious life" involved; and one can guess what kind of story Solomon told about policemen and prisons. Ross's acquaintances must have included all of the prominent homosexuals in late Victorian England. He was an intimate of Oscar Wilde, as well as Lord Alfred Douglas and Aubrey Beardsley. Undoubtedly his later relations with Wilde, whom he tried to help, explain the comment about "wastrels with the artistic temperament" who turn against friends and those who have assisted them. As to his having himself "remained reputable," the phrasing of this comment from his 1909 book *Masques & Phases* suggests that this is just how he wanted to be thought of. Even that late, sympathy for the sexual outcast still had for safety's sake to be tempered with a tone of moral superiority toward the "sordid" and the "vicious."

Finally, there is no evidence that Simeon Solomon ever became a Roman Catholic. The rumors to that effect may derive from his having received Catholic charity late in his life and from his having produced so many pictures—the *Mystery of Faith* for one—that represented Catholic subjects. (So did Rossetti, who was certainly not a practicing Christian.)

He died in his sixties, in 1905 at St. Giles's Workhouse.

In a limited sense, the life of Solomon anticipates the life of Wilde. But Oscar Wilde was much more brilliant, even more foolish, very much more vulnerable. He also had the bad luck to be prosecuted after the writing of the new and repressive sex laws of the 1880s.

Wilde's story is too well-known to need repeating in detail. Son of a distinguished Irish family—his mother wrote under the name of "Speranza" and his father was a surgeon in Dublin, where Oscar was born—Wilde became something of a dandy and eccentric at Oxford, wrote and spoke on behalf of "art for art's sake," the new French aesthetic idea first made current in England by James Whistler; in 1884, at the age of thirty, he married Constance Lloyd; he wrote modern fairy tales and plays, including *The Importance of Being Earnest* (1895), the only first-rate play produced by any nineteenth-century British writer. He also fell in love, after his marriage, with Lord Alfred Douglas, a beautiful, blond, clever, extremely neurotic and unscrupulous young man who translated his *Salome* (1893), the supposedly scandalous play that Wilde wrote in French for Sarah Bernhardt. Douglas was widely regarded as a dissolute, but his father, the Marquis of Queensberry, blamed Wilde for his son's behavior and publicly insulted him (for "posing as a somdomite"[*sic*]). It may have been brave but it was certainly foolish of Wilde to respond with a libel action. The upshot was a trial in which, under the recent law, he was convicted of immoral acts and sentenced to two years' imprisonment. He left prison in 1897 and died three years later, in Paris.

These are the bare bones of the story. There is no doubt that Wilde loved Douglas—who was, as André Gide later observed, a cruel, selfish, and unworthy object for his affection—and that the two had a sexual affair. In this connection, and in his relations with others whom he loved, liked, or admired, Wilde was generous. He was pained, for instance, when in 1891 Edmond de Goncourt was quoted as saying,

> Le poète anglais Wilde me disait, ce soir, que le seul Anglais qui avait lu Balzac à l'heure actuelle était Swinburne. Et ce Swinburne, il me montre comme un fanfaron du vice, qui avait tout fait pour faire croire ses concitoyens à sa pédérastie, à sa bestialité, sans être le moins du monde pédéraste ni bestialitaire.

Wilde at once protested to Goncourt about having his name connected to this comment on Swinburne's "pretended" pederasty— and he objected to the comment itself. (It seems odd that both Swinburne and Wilde were accused of affecting homosexuality when, with at least one of them, it was no affectation at all.) This concern for Swinburne, whom he admired, suggests an attractive side to Wilde. And, much as Robert Ross may have felt put upon by his petulance, even paranoia, in the prison days and after, Wilde—who surely had a great deal to resent, beginning with the callowness of Douglas—displayed remarkable humanity in those terrible days. He wrote long letters to the journals about cruel treatment of the feebleminded and of children (infants of six or eight years could be remanded to a prison), and these letters were a factor in the reforming of a particularly brutal and mindless penal system. Bankrupt, disgraced, deserted by his wife and family, neglected even by the one for whose sake he was suffering, he retained a moral sense much more impressive than —and very much in contrast with—that of the moralizers who condemned him.

The best account of his ordeal is found in his own letters (edited by Rupert Hart-Davis). That account ends, of course, with his death in 1900. But the story of what Wilde's trial meant,

what its implications were, goes beyond that—goes well into the
twentieth century.

For the Victorian scandalmonger, things must have seeeemed
to be going from bad to worse—or from good to better. Swinburne's poetry was shocking, but there was nothing definitely
known about his behavior. Burton wrote about, had actually
visited, male bordellos; and people wondered. Solomon was arrested *in flagrante delicto.* Not only were Wilde's sins proved
against him (and he, a married man); he was imprisoned for
them. In the 1890s, after the Wilde trial, there was an almost hysterical reaction to the idea of sexual deviation. Aesthetes became
suspect, and *The Yellow Book,* a periodical with which Wilde
and aestheticism were connected for no very good reason, suffered. Self-righteousness and hypocrisy appeared to have reached
a new high.

By the mid-1890s, Burton was dead, Solomon was on the
streets, and Swinburne was in the suburbs. Wilde, in prison, still
had friends—including the loyal Ada and Ernest Leverson—but
the world at large appeared to have turned its back on him with
loathing.

Yet the trial and its aftermath, paradoxically, marked the
beginning of a public awareness that would eventually alter attitudes toward a sort of sexual behavior not even to be spoken of
earlier. During the trial, there were a few sane voices raised
against the hysteria of Queensberry, the newspapers, and the
courts. One of them, surprisingly, was that of the very same Robert
Buchanan who had attacked Swinburne and Rossetti in his 1871
"Fleshly School of Poetry." Buchanan wrote to the *Star* asking
for some Christian charity in "this land of Christian shibboleths
and formulas" and concluded,

> Let us ask ourselves ... who are casting these stones, and
> whether they are those "without sin amongst us" or those
> who are themselves notoriously corrupt.

To this rather startling question—especially startling if we consider that the Biblical phrase was applied in the gospel of John
to hypocrisy about sex—Queensberry replied by asking, "Is Mr.
Buchanan himself without sin?" (Each seemed to be asking if the
other had not had some homosexual experience.) Even the un-

reliable Alfred Douglas, Wilde's beloved "Bosie," performed creditably with a letter to the press about the trial judge—who had declared that "he knew of no graver offense than that with which Mr. Wilde is charged"—pointing out that this offense (supposedly graver than treason or murder) was in law a misdemeanor punishable at most by two years' imprisonment.

Over the years such voices were to sound more often. There was more than half a century between Wilde and Wolfenden—and the report advising a reform in sex laws which would finally make such a case as Wilde's impossible. But a counterreaction to the late-Victorian overreaction inevitably came. Tragic and terrible as the ordeal was, the whole affair had its value. Not only did it make discussion of sexual offenses possible; it made more and yet more people reflect on the rationality, the humanity, of sex laws that could wreck the life of a man of genius.

Swinburne lived longer than the others. He had made the most ado about sexual deviation—in his poetry, where it was safe to do so—and he had been in fact the most timid of these men. Solomon was forgotten, Burton's reputation remained dubious, and Wilde's name was a scandal for the many, a rallying cry for the few. When Swinburne, the outrageous iconoclast of the 1860s, died in the first decade of this century, he was a Grand Old Man of English literature.

5
An
End and
Some
Beginnings

In the long years liker must they grow;
The man be more of woman, she of man;
He gain in sweetness and in moral height,
Nor lose the wrestling thews that throw the world;
She mental breadth, nor fail in childward care,
Nor lose the childlike in the larger mind;
Till at the last she set herself to man,
Like perfect music unto noble words;
And so these twain, upon the skirts of Time,
Sit side by side, full-summed in all their powers,
Dispensing harvest, sowing the To-be,
Self-reverent each and reverencing each,
Distinct in individualities,
But like each other even as those who love.
Then comes the statelier Eden back to men:
Then reign the world's great bridals, chaste and calm:
Then springs the crowning race of humankind.
May these things be!

(Alfred Tennyson, 1847)

There is no reason that all human existence should be con-
structed on some one or some small number of patterns . . .
a person['s] . . .own mode of laying out his existence is the best,
not because it is the best in itself, but because it is his own
mode. . . . But the man, and still more the woman, who can be
accused either of doing "what nobody does," or of not doing
"what everybody does," is the subject of as much depreciatory
remark as if he or she had committed some grave moral de-
linquency. . . .
The demand that all other people shall resemble ourselves
grows by what it feeds on. If resistance waits till life is *nearly*
one uniform type, all deviations from that type will come to
be considered impious, immoral, even monstrous and contrary
to nature.

(John Stuart Mill, 1859)

Our temporary world . . . supposes it possible for a woman to
be mentally active up to the point of spiritual clarity and also
fleshly vile; a guide to life and a biter at the fruits of death. . . .
It has not yet been taught to appreciate a quality certifying to
sound citizenship.

(George Meredith, 1885)

The grotesque sexual compacts made between men and women
under marriage laws . . . represent to some of us a political
necessity . . . to some a divine ordinance, to some a romantic
ideal, to some a domestic profession for women, and to some
that worst of blundering abominations, an institution which society has outgrown but not modified, and which "advanced" in-
dividuals are therefore forced to evade.

(George Bernard Shaw, 1898)

When, to begin with, we considered reasons for the Victorian—and modern—preoccupation with sex, a number of these came up: industrialization and the tendency of people to lose close personal ties with family and neighborhood; the urban crowding and poverty that encouraged prostitution; the spread of literacy and freer ideas about sexual behavior among the working class as well as the middle class; and the increasing loss of firm religious faith.

There may be other reasons or, rather, another way of putting this complex of reasons. The Victorians had, as to a great extent we have, a compulsion to define themselves. The need for self-definition extended to the nation and to the age itself. If, as some historians say, the writing of history began with the Romantic period, then surely the sense of there being periods that we can define (and not just chronicle) virtually began with the Victorians. And the first thing they were concerned about was their own period. They were the first to name their own times;

Elizabethans never called themselves by that name, but Victorians wrote about "this Victorian age." More than that, with their
concern for "The Spirit of the Age" and the "Signs of the Times"
(titles used by Mill and Carlyle), Victorian writers invented the
cliché about "an age of transition." They applied that phrase, ap-
propriately, to their own historical era. It was, of course, a time
of rapid change; they were the generations in between the older,
stable world of social institutions hardly changed since the late
Middle Ages (the church, the universities, the laws about money,
land, and marriage) and what we think of as the modern world.

But what has all this to do with sex?

Self-definition does begin with the self. The attempts by
Victorian poets to understand their own beings are often quite
direct and clear: Gerard Manley Hopkins, writing late in the century, and partly at least in reaction to his own intense homosexual feelings, strove to define himself as a creature, an immortal
soul; Matthew Arnold, disillusioned with religion and philosophy ("Weary of myself, and sick of asking/What I am, and what
I ought to be"), tried in "Dover Beach" to define his true self
through the idea of sexual love, in the dramatic plea, "Ah, love,
let us be true/To one another!" And for other Victorians, not
just the poets, self-definition involved sex.

Writing in prose, Arnold attacked John Stuart Mill's old
friend John Roebuck for his smug comments upon the "unri-
valled happiness" of mid-Victorian Englishmen by citing the
newspaper account of a young woman who, just out of the Not-
tingham workhouse, had strangled her own illegitimate child.

> And "our unrivalled happiness";—what an element of
> grimness, bareness, and hideousness mixes with it and blurs
> it; the workhouse, the dismal Mapperly Hills ... the gloom,
> the smoke, the strangled illegitimate child! "I ask you
> whether, the world over or in past history, there is anything
> like it?" [Roebuck's words] Perhaps not, one is inclined to
> answer; but at any rate, in that case, the world is very
> much to be pitied. And the final touch,—short, bleak and
> inhuman: *Wragg is in custody.* The sex lost in the confu-
> sion of our unrivalled happiness? ...

This powerfully ironic passage suggests not only a contempt for
mindless and heartless self-congratulation but also a sense that

being a self, being a person, involves having a name *and* a sex.

Social changes and religious uncertainties combined in the nineteenth century to make this aspect of personal identity increasingly important. There are levels of self-definition. One can be first of all a creature, a creation of God; then, a child, a product of parents whose (father's) name one bears; then, a member of a class or group or tradition (and this may mean being a cobbler because one is the child of a cobbler) ; then, a female or male, girl or boy, woman or man. For many Victorians, the theory of Creation and therefore of their being creatures was in grave doubt; the relation of children to parents, with increasing mobility both spatial and social, was less clear and comforting (and less constraining) ; the social shifts in such families as the Ruskins, Mills, and Merediths were so extreme within a generation that a cobbler's son might be a self-made gentleman, if a nervous one; and what was left was sex. That is to say, women and men might feel it necessary to prove their value, their identity, by demonstrating their sexuality; the compulsion is distinctly modern, but its origins are Victorian.

And the more sensitive Victorians were aware of this.

Sex had become a frightening force, as the extremes in prudery and hypocrisy would indicate, just because it had become a force so strong, so central, so essential to the psychic life of men and women in the nineteenth century.

Prudery, hypocrisy, could not forever both express and mask the problem. The last decades of the nineteenth century and the first years of the twentieth represent a turning point: the end of a transitional era and the beginning of the modern world. At the conclusion of the Victorian era, a number of ideas were in the air, a number of revolutionary ideas about the arts, society, and sex. These were ideas that had rarely been expressed before the 1880s—or, at least, had almost never been fully articulated.

With the work of artists like Aubrey Beardsley and critics like Walter Pater and John Symonds, in this so-called decadent time, came a new emphasis on earthly, physical experience—and on personal, emotional impressions as well—that signalled a break with the moralizing of John Ruskin and his disciples. It was not a total break. Ruskin himself in later years came to ad-

mire the beauty of Renaissance art, even of nudes, and he greatly
modified his earlier Calvinistic tone as he grew more interested
in the ethics of human relations and less imprisoned in the
patriarchal morality, the largely anti-sexual code of his parents.
But Ruskin could go only so far. He was an old man. And the
breezy manner of that foremost advocate of "art for art's sake,"
the American painter James McNeill Whistler (actually, Swinburne was the first to use the phrase in England, in his 1868 *William Blake*), exasperated him so that Ruskin called the artist "a
coxcomb [who asks] two hundred guineas for flinging a pot of
paint in the public's face." His reference was to a Whistler painting, but the comment was almost certainly inspired as much by
what Whistler said as by how he painted. Gleefully, the American sued for libel. The ensuing trial was a seriocomic reflection
of what was happening in the world of arts and letters at the end
of the 1870s. To be sure, Whistler quarreled with almost everyone, including his sometime friends Swinburne and Wilde: he
took exception to the critical remarks of the one and accused the
other of plagiarizing him. Furthermore, his basic criticism of
Ruskin, that he regarded painting as merely a form of literature,
had been anticipated by a number of others, including Sir
Charles Eastlake and his clever wife Lady Eastlake (in her devas-
tating 1856 review of *Modern Painters*). But there was a special
symbolic quality to the Ruskin-Whistler trial: it was a conflict, or
so it must have seemed, between the old morality of art and the
new assertion of artistic freedom. And it ushered in the last two
decades of the century. As even Whistler's 1890 *Gentle Art of
Making Enemies* reveals, nobody really won—though technically
he won his libel suit. But in a sense, the aging Ruskin lost; his
right to speak with absolute authority on matters artistic was not
only questioned but laughed at. Swinburne, Wilde, Whistler, and
"art for art's sake" were to have their day.

The popular version of that French doctrine included the assumption that artists and writers were not subject to the moral
conventions governing ordinary people—that is, the sexual rules.
Some artists and writers, clearly, shared that assumption. Even after 1895 and the Wilde trial, even well into the twentieth cen-

tury, "artistic temperament" and sexual freedom were thought to go together.

The more serious point is that all the arts, including literature as well as painting, were gradually being freed to represent some facts of life, not just to tell pretty stories or preach the received morals. In their very different ways, George Eliot and James Whistler were both championing the right—actually, the duty—of the artist to show things as they are really seen, not as they have traditionally been represented. (In fact, since this was Ruskin's original doctrine as well—he pointed out that skies were sometimes green—it was sadly ironic that the defender of Joseph Turner in the 1840s should become the hysterical antagonist of Whistler in the late 1870s.) This meant, in part, the right and duty to be honest about sex.

In the novel, it meant the sexual honesty of George Meredith and of Thomas Hardy, and—what was even more distressing to some—the treatment by George Moore in his *Esther Waters* (1894) of a poor girl who is seduced and deserted, has an illegitimate child and, like Matthew Arnold's Wragg, is forced into the workhouse. Moore was directly influenced by the realism of the French novel, as both his relatively sordid subject matter and his hard, literal style would indicate. As we saw, the general Victorian response to French realism, especially that of Émile Zola, was horrified fascination. Moore's subject in *Esther Waters* was no more overtly sexual and no more sordid than Hardy's in *Tess of the d'Urbervilles* (published three years earlier) or *Jude the Obscure* (published two years later); but the impression he gave of being "French"—and even Zola-esque—made the book seem even more shocking.

Meredith's later novels were disturbing in a different but related way, for he raised serious questions in them about sexual roles and marriage—in effect, the questions we saw raised in his much earlier poetry.

That earlier poetry reminds us that although the agitation for women's rights surfaced near the end of the nineteenth century with a widespread demand for the vote, the suffrage campaign in the 1890s and the first decade of this century was in fact a climax to a larger, older, and less obvious movement. It was a movement with roots in the ideas of Mary Wollstonecraft; and its earlier effects are evident not only in the lives and works of Robert Owen and William Thompson, of Harriet Taylor and John Stuart Mill, of George Eliot and George Meredith, but also in the writing of the Brontë sisters and even in the verse of Alfred Tennyson, whose fantasy, *The Princess,* has to do with the founding of a woman's college. Unorganized until almost the end of the period, this was nevertheless a genuine movement in the sense of a tendency and influence; it involved pressure for the rights of women to own property (married women could not), to achieve a higher education and career, to divorce for cause and not be both socially and legally ruined as a result. All these issues preceded the one of suffrage.

One of the most interesting aspects of this movement is the psychology of its opposition: the ostensible grounds and the putative motives of those men—and women, too—who on each of those issues were not just against but were profoundly afraid of change.

John Stuart Mill's father, James the Benthamite, simply thought women's rights were adequately protected by the powers of their husbands and fathers. (He also thought workers' rights were adequately seen to by their employers.) The later opponent of women's having property, education, careers, and self-determination usually presented an emotional argument: the result would be to make women "unfeminine." Along with this went the old argument that if (middle-class) women did not remain cloistered in the home—and garden—the family would collapse and thus all social order would be threatened. But the assumption regarding what was "feminine" and "unfeminine," if not more basic, is more revealing about general attitudes toward sexual identification.

It raises some interesting questions. Were a great many men afraid that a clear distinction between feminine and masculine might be lost—so that if women were no longer feminine, men would no longer seem to be distinctly masculine? The question involves what Kate Millett calls sexual politics but also the fear of losing sexual identity which, for a male, means fear of castra-

tion. The equation of female independence with male effeminacy
—if not impotency—is made explicit by the bully-boy males in
several mid-Victorian works, by the stupid and blustering father
in Tennyson's *Princess,* and by the equally coarse two uncles of
the protagonist in Swinburne's *Atalanta.* In this age of so much
social change and uncertainty a good many women, too, could
feel threatened by the possibility of losing their comfortably self-
defining sexual role; if a man could be unmanned, a woman
could be "unwomanned."

But, to go further: just what did it mean, to those who felt
and argued this way, for a woman to be womanly?

No doubt, the answer would depend in part upon the
woman's social class. If she was of the middle class, or of even
higher status, she might be expected to be passive, chaste, available as a wife but otherwise charmingly remote. If she was a
servant girl, depending on the household and the man who was
asked, she might be expected to be a chaste as well as attentive
person—or, instead, a compliant object of sexual interest.

There tended to be the two possibilities, the familiar polar
opposites, that might be called "feminine." One, we saw, was
symbolized in poetry and art by the angel or the lily: the pure
female, a version perhaps of St. Mary that combined elements of
purity and motherhood. The other was represented by the harlot
or the rose: the female as a sexual target, sometimes imagined as
a deer or other animal to be hunted and tamed. Of course, the extreme polarizing occurs with the madonna-harlot syndrome we
found represented seriously in Tennyson, Rossetti, and Swinburne, and parodied by Meredith.

For a woman to be (like George Eliot) neither a lily nor a
rose, neither a madonna nor a harlot, for a woman thus to escape
from such stereotyping was for her to be unwomanly.

There was probably no way to answer irrational objections
to women's having rights—no effective mode of allaying deep-
seated sexual fears. But feminists could and did play upon the
contradiction within the very conception of what was feminine
by raising a moral issue no earnest Victorian could entirely
avoid. This was, once more, the issue of prostitution. They could
point out that women were not born as lilies or roses, as saints or

wantons, but that circumstances changed virgins into whores. The circumstances were, above all, economic and they were reinforced by laws that forced unprotected women into one version or another of prostitution. Prostitution in mid- and late-Victorian England proved to be the best grounds for their arguments that women could find—moral grounds both in the more puritanical sense and in the sense that people who disliked the work were forced into it, and into humiliation. It provided the grounds to argue that for many a woman to be "feminine" could only mean for her to be, for the most part unwillingly, a whore.

As Michael Pearson's recent study, *The Five Pound Virgins*, shows, the growing crusade against prostitution at the end of the century represented a combination of forces: the Quakers, the Salvation Army, and the press, especially the *Pall Mall Gazette*; it included as well a number of feminists, and what it revealed could only help the feminist cause.

What it revealed was a shocking array of facts: child prostitutes (thirteen was the age of consent for a girl, but many were younger; and in case of trouble the police and courts prosecuted the twelve-year-old whore, *not* the middle-aged man who bought and used her) ; mothers who sold their daughters into brothels; and white slavery, lurid as it sounds, which made a sizable profit exporting girls to the continent. In the 1870s, Rossetti had been condemned for writing in "Jenny" about a prostitute. But by the 1890s, given the clearly moral tone of this crusade, only the most obtuse could insist that the matter be left unmentioned. There were, however, still plenty of the most obtuse about.

Many earlier objections to the traffic in prostitutes, we saw, had to do largely if not exclusively with the danger to men. This was true of Newman's attack. Now it became impossible to ignore the workings of a double standard that was both moral and economic, to pretend that, while the men who went to whores and mistresses simply required relief, the fallen women were lewd, seductive beasts who freely chose their way of life.

All the evidence revealed that few of them had any choice at all.

We observed that George Bernard Shaw struck just this note in his play about prostitution, *Mrs. Warren's Profession,* and that

the subject was considered too improper for the play to be produced at all. The familiar and ubiquitous fact of life was too
painful to recognize openly on the stage—even if one were forced
to see it and actually read about it in the newspapers.

Shaw's work was not only about recognized prostitution,
however. It was meant first of all as an attack upon capitalism;
the madame—Mrs. Warren—and her financial backers were presented as capitalists who grew rich from the prostitution of
others. This is the reason Mrs. Warren's daughter, Vivie, rejects
her mother—not because the older woman was once forced into
being a prostitute in order to live but because she accepted and
became a part of the order which caused this to happen. Vivie is
one of the earliest examples in Shaw of that figure he derived in
part from Henrik Ibsen and developed in the English play (as
Meredith did in the novel), the new woman who rejects the
"doll's house" to which she is confined by a conventional marriage and, ultimately, the whole imprisoning environment of
which that marriage is a part. Although Shaw's socialism was,
strictly speaking, no more Marxist than that of the British Labor
Party, he tended to agree with Marx that in the West at the end
of the nineteenth century, it was rare for any sexual relation in
or out of marriage not to be a kind of prostitution.

According to Robert Owen's formula, sex without love was
prostitution and sex with love was true marriage. Strictly speaking, that would mean that a number of legal marriages involved
the relation of prostitute and client—and that some unorthodox
liaisons, including even some homosexual liaisons like Wilde's,
were in the true sense marriages.

But even by the end of the century, that was not a view
which could be very widely expressed. Women had achieved
some of their earlier goals with the founding of women's colleges
(beginning in the 1850s) and with such reforms of the marriage
laws as the Married Woman's Property Act in the 1880s; they
were on the way to achieving suffrage. Suffrage, but not yet true
equality, for the movement toward that point where they could
defined first of all not by sex but by common humanity was still
only a movement. If this was true of women in general, it was
much more true of all who engaged in deviant sexual behavior.

To most people it still seemed that so-called deviants, specifically homosexuals, were defining themselves sexually and in a perverse way by behaving as the opposite sex was meant to behave.

Not only in the eyes of the law (since Victoria disbelieved in lesbianism) but also in the usual view of the public, male homosexuality was far worse than female. Paradoxically, that was true not at all because women were allowed more sexual freedom but because women were often regarded—by men and by themselves in many instances—as lesser beings. The sequence of assumptions was likely to be, first, that males who are sexually interested in other males thus act as if they were females; second, that females are intrinsically inferior to males because they are both physically and intellectually weaker; and third, that therefore homosexual males are denying their own sexual identity in favor of a lesser identity, and by so doing, are being traitors to the higher and better station into which they were born—that is, to manhood.

Such men also threatened their fellows—threatened not only quite literally to seduce other men but also to introduce disturbing sexual possibilities. The tone of the popular and journalistic responses to the Oscar Wilde trial was unmistakably one of fear—a fear, perhaps, that the loss of sexual identity in the stable, conventional, and typifying sense, might mean the loss of human dignity. We read a great deal about the late Victorian crisis of faith and of how Darwin's hypothesis, other scientific developments in geology and anthropology, and the Biblical "higher criticism" all shook and frightened thoughtful men and women. If it is true that sex tended to replace religion as the central interest and way of self-identification for the later Victorians, then the changes in female status and the attacks upon a sexual status quo—but, above all, such scandals as the Solomon and Wilde trials—would be once again unsettling, even terrifying.

And all the more so because, far from introducing any novel facts about sex, these events only threatened to reveal some very well-known but rarely acknowledged truths.

Male homosexual behavior, for example, was almost certainly familiar not just in the very lowest orders, not just in the British Navy—where it was a fact of life—and not just in the public schools for boys. It seems striking how casually both anal and oral intercourse among men is taken in Victorian pornography. (It may be a joke or an oddity, but it is neither horrifying nor, it seems, so rare; and for the characters in these stories, an occasional homosexual experience is not inconsistent with a great deal of heterosexual whoring.)

It has, in fact, been argued that male homosexuality increased enormously in England near the end of the nineteenth century. This is another one of those points that cannot be proved or disproved. But the life of Lytton Strachey, as documented in Michael Holroyd's two-volume biography, shows how astonishingly prevalent mutual sex was among young men in the late Victorian and early modern universities. One has the impression that at Cambridge, at least, it was rather exceptional for a bright and reasonably attractive male undergraduate not to be involved more or less sexually with another young man, or a tutor, or perhaps even a distinguished professor. And there were plenty of brilliant and eminent men, beginning with the father of modern economics, Maynard Keynes, who appeared to have vied with each other for the more handsome students! (Keynes and Strachey were in love with the same young man at one point, and both made a number of conquests.) A good deal of the wooing, to be sure, went hardly further than a kiss and an embrace. It is, however, hard to believe that there was not fairly often more than that going on in such an environment.

If all of this was so, why the hypocrisy, the fear of sexual oddity, the hysterical condemnation of Wilde?

Again, the answer is that the fear and hysteria occurred precisely because all of this was so. In Lytton Strachey's own work there is something of that nervousness about being identified with the sexual outcast.

Strachey's most popular book was his *Eminent Victorians,* published in 1918, which includes biographical sketches of such sitting ducks as Thomas Arnold and Florence Nightingale. It was the book that pretty much began the twentieth-century tradition of condescending with amusement—or condemning out of hand —all things Victorian, and especially Victorian hypocrisy. Some of the very latest illustrated books on Victorian customs, pictures,

taste, and sexual mores show that this fifty-year-old pose of superiority, although boringly predictable, is still not dead. Just how
superior we are in the 1970s to "the Victorians"—generally referred to as a monolithic group without distinctions of class, sex,
decade, or intelligence—is very questionable even though, like
Lytton Strachey, we are too smug to recognize the question.

How often, for example, are most of us as hypocritical as
most of them—and as Strachey—about sexual roles and sexual
behavior? The question sounds Victorian in that it implies a
moral condemnation of our age; it is meant only to suggest a
point, the point that on matters of sex we may not be so completely unlike our cultural ancestors as we suppose.

Ours, too, is a sex-obsessed period, for we inherit Victorian
compulsiveness about, *and* fear of, the sexual. The young girl
whose ankle had to be covered a hundred years ago is succeeded
inevitably by the topless waitress. The sexual eccentric who was
then called unnatural is now called sick, and sometimes the latter
word carries just as much condemnation—since, for us, so-called
emotional sickness can be the equivalent of sin.

Or, rather, it can be worse.

At least those Victorians who were thought to be living in
sin were also recognized as having made their choice. And the
sinner was, according to the Bible, a person of infinite value.
The greatest Victorian sexual rebels were not orthodox Christians but they drew on traditional religious ideas—often, the notion of sin as mainly a matter of sex—in order to reinterpret
them. Often they implied, if they did not say openly, that sexual
sins were not the worst.

What was more important than loose sexual behavior? As
sins, pride in the form of smugness and lying in the form of hypocrisy. As virtues, love and honesty. In one way or another,
this is what Mill, Browning, Meredith, Eliot, Dickens, and perhaps finally, even Wilde said.

In effect, they were attacking not religion and certainly not
sex but the false relation between religious values—if you like,
Christian ethics—and sexuality. To put it another way (but not
the way any one of them would have put it), they were challeng-

ing the confusion of sex with soul, of sexual identity—womanli-
ness or manhood—with human value.

Modern journalists like to write about the supposedly anti-
Victorian sexual revolution in our times. That phrase covers a
good many developments and tendencies; and, like some other
revolutions that have filled newspaper pages in the past few
years, it may be almost as much the invention as the discovery of
the feature writers. But no doubt there have been some changes
in our publicly stated and publicly acceptable attitudes toward
sex during these years.

For one thing, we talk about sexuality, about acts and organs, as people rarely did some time ago. The demand for candor
about what once were called the facts of life can imply any one of
several attitudes. One is tolerance of pornography and approval
of sex education. But opposed to this tolerance there can be an
insistence on the private nature of sex—on the unfairness of its
being made public, being exploited. The insistence on this principle, that sexual activity is private, has led to agitation against
laws that proscribe adultery, homosexuality, and abortion.

Sexual issues today, then, are not really so clear-cut as the
phrase "sexual revolution" might suggest. One person may take a
so-called revolutionary stance on Issue A and quite the opposite
on Issue B—depending on who runs which revolution. For example, a woman who is trying to free herself from female stereo-
types, from excessive role-playing, may object strongly to the
toleration of pornography that reduces women to sexual organs
or "pieces," mere usable sex objects (and pornography tends to
do this), while a man who approves of sexual openness, of birth
control, and of abortion, may intensely dislike the minimizing of
social-sexual contrasts between the sexes. Each is, in a different
sense, part radical and part conservative or at least nonrevolu-
tionary by somebody else's definition.

By contrast, the Victorian revolution in sexual attitudes did
have a single, central tendency: that was to recognize the reality
of sex (in various forms) and thus, odd as this may seem, to *reduce* its importance in human life!

None of the earlier revolutionary Victorians went so far as

Bertrand Russell, with his famous comment that having sexual intercourse need be no more significant than having afternoon tea. None of them was uninterested in or casual about sex. But such writers as Eliot, Mill, and Meredith clearly believed that there were facts and values more important yet, including human dignity.

If Victorian prudery as well as Victorian prostitution and pornography were signs of being obsessed by sex, then it was exactly against this obsession that some Victorians rebelled. Above all, they rebelled against the hypocrite who was often prude and pander at once.

Each of the major issues, then, in the history of Victorian sexual debate, criticism, and agitation, involves a need to reduce the fact of sex from the enormous proportions it had assumed by the middle of the nineteenth century to more rational proportions. This meant refusing to see sex as a religion, either as Coventry Patmore did or as those fearful people did who thought the very subject sacred and unnameable, involving angels, saints, and demons. (The tendency to translate a myth of the fallen man into that of the sexually fallen woman is instructive.) It meant refusing to see sex as the sole or even the most basic determinant of human identity and human value, refusing to believe that it was more important to be manly than to love, more important to be womanly than to think.

What were those major issues, those areas in which sensitive and articulate Victorians wanted to replace an unspoken quasi-religious myth with fact, sympathy, and reason? First, the laws and customs governing marriage and divorce. Second, and closely related, the legal, political, and finally economic status of women, married or not. Third, the conduct of any person's sex life when it involved consenting adults—whether that life was adulterous, homosexual, or in other ways irregular.

In Chapter 2 we considered briefly the attacks made early in the nineteenth century on indissoluble marriage and the less direct but no less powerful criticisms implied by the fiction of George Eliot, of Charles Dickens, and of course, of George Meredith and Thomas Hardy. We saw that Hardy's *Jude*, in particular, denied the necessity for a sacramental yoking of sex and religion.

In Victorian poetry, too, there were attacks upon conventional marriage and specifically upon the idea of its being divine. Robert Browning's young wife Pompilia in *The Ring and the Book,* his masterpiece, says that in heaven there is no marriage and that marriage on earth is a counterfeit of love. And Tennyson's familiar phrase "marriages are made in heaven" is a bitterly ironic one in the context; it comes from "Aylmer's Field," one of his poems about false "mammon-marriage" in a commercial age —and it is meant to represent a silly sentimentality that is blind to the fact of what most middle-class marriages were, how and why they were made. All of these and many, many other literary works were part of the movement that was finally to establish sexual relations as secular bonds subject to dissolution.

A good deal has been said about the larger movement for women's rights. Here, too, it was necessary to challenge the sacredness and thus the primacy of biological sex—to challenge the religion of woman-worship as well as the subsidiary myth of woman as incarnate sin. This problem was and is much subtler, much more difficult, because these attitudes were so pervasive in the middle of the nineteenth century and because they could hardly be changed directly through legal action. By the 1890s, however, enough women had established themselves in the larger world to make it more difficult for any man *or* woman to perpetuate the idea of the female angel—or devil. It became difficult to think of a secretary or a writer or a political antagonist with whom one actually debated as quite angelic or totally fallen. The great woman writers of the nineteenth century had helped to change the situation: the Brontës, George Eliot, Elizabeth Browning, Elizabeth Gaskell, even the shy Christina Rossetti. Some men dramatized the change: George Meredith, Thomas Hardy, and finally E. M. Forster, in their novels.

The mention of Forster brings up a curious fact, that is, the frequent affinity between feminist goals and those of male homosexuals. The point is not that women and homosexual men shared what much of the world thought of as "feminine" qualities, but that all suffered from a sexual stereotyping that reduced them from human beings with individuality to what we might now call simply broads or faggots. Once more, the problem was to establish that basic identity, basic value, is not synonymous with either biological sex or sexual preference, that sex is just not all *that* important.

Only generally significant matters, those that directly affect society as a whole, could rationally be thought to come under the jurisdiction of civil law: this was the argument of secularists like John Stuart Mill. The position, spelled out even more clearly in Mill's essay *On Liberty* than in his earlier volume *The Subjection of Women,* meant that private sexual affairs should remain entirely private. Neither the law nor the church should be involved.

In sum, one can say that the prominent Victorians who rebelled against the sexual narrowness and obsessiveness of their age by what they wrote, said, *and* did, were denying the assumption that sex is divine, sacramental, mystical, *or* sinful.

They had in many respects a harder job than any modern sexual revolutionaries: they suffered ostracism, persecution, prison—and ill health, neurosis, intermittent guilt. And it may have seemed by the end of the age that, after all, not much had been altered of the middle-class, middle-brow, mid-Victorian repressions and hypocrisies, so slowly and subtly did the changes in popular feeling occur.

Not one of these major Victorians lived to see the first publication of D. H. Lawrence in 1911, and it may have been just as well. A late Victorian himself by birth, Lawrence has been hailed or condemned as the great rebel against sexual decorum, the man who dealt honestly with sexual acts and sexual drives. James Joyce used four-letter words in print before Lawrence, but incidentally; and no early modern writer concentrated so much on sex as Lawrence did. An erratic genius, he became best-known, or most notorious, for some of his worst work—notably *Lady Chatterley's Lover,* sometimes called "Lady Loverly's Chatter," in which the Anglo-Saxon words and displays of penis and pudendum have distracted a good many readers (and legal authorities) from a hackneyed story. From the point of view of a Mill or a Meredith, he would represent not sexual radicalism but sexual reaction—that is, regression to something not wholly unlike the mystique of Coventry Patmore.

If, as was suggested, our own world shares a good deal of the Victorian compulsiveness about sex, a compulsive fascination that tends to mechanize and dehumanize sexual objects and acts, along with a compulsive fear expressed in hypocrisy, the fact is demonstrated not only in our pop art and pornography but also is our serious art and writing—beginning with Lawrence.

Of course, in at least one respect Lawrence was within the tradition of Victorian realism: he did try to be honest in his observations and he never blinked at the physical or psychological aspects of sex—far from it. But his psychology tended to merge into sexual mysticism; his men and women tended to become embodiments of sheer sexual force, an elemental and ultimately inhuman force. If sex was not for him quite a religion, it seems to have been a quasi-religious, a demonic, power. He was capable at times—consistent with this largely Victorian attitude toward sex —of depicting men as divine bulls and women as sacred cows.

Among contemporary writers, Lawrence's most prominent successors have been Henry Miller and Norman Mailer. Mailer is the best example of how Victorian obsession with sex has been translated into our modern obsession—translated and not, essentially, changed very much.

For Mailer's attitude is, again, quasi-religious on matters of marriage (or its equivalent) ; the role and rights of women; and sexual deviation.

Significantly, although his background is not Christian, Mailer tends to identify himself with that tradition (in *Cannibals and Christians*) , and his language becomes that of sacramental religion when he writes of the sexual relation between man and woman. That may seem odd because his language in such passages also includes short "dirty" words for the sex act and organs. But he is trying to consecrate those words—which for him are not obscene—just as, he believes, the actions and objects they represent are sacred. In this sense, sexual intercourse, the marriage of male and female bodies, should be and is at best sacramental (one is again reminded of Patmore) .

As for women, Mailer's comments are well known; some have been made on television. They correspond almost perfectly to the "madonna-harlot" syndrome so familiar in Victorian life and literature. That is, women are either goddesses or low beasts —to use not Patmore's or the later Tennyson's words, but Mailer's own. Again, if a woman is not a religious figure who is thus spiritually superior to a man—madonna, angel, great mother, or goddess—she can only be a fallen and subhuman being. There is no human in-between.

Finally, Mailer is inclined to be disdainful—at best—of any sexual activity other than that between man and woman, penis and vagina. It is not only the homosexual relation that is involved; he becomes harsher in condemning masturbation, just as Lawrence did. Nothing should replace—and that is distinctly a moral *should*—the sacrament of male-and-female genital intercourse.

Clearly, if Norman Mailer is any part of a twentieth-century sexual revolution, his part represents the precise antithesis of what the Victorian sexual revolution stood for. The four-letter words only mask that fact.

But then Mailer, partly inverting and largely continuing the popular Victorian attitudes toward sex, also represents the antithesis of what other modern sexual revolutionaries stand for— those who advocate reform in sex laws, an end to sexual stereotyping of men as well as women, and a degree of freedom for sexual minorities.

These are the rebels who belong in the secular tradition of George Eliot, George Meredith, Harriet Taylor, and John Stuart Mill. What those Victorians voiced a hundred years ago and more was a set of ideas about freedom that are now again being voiced. The women's groups and others agitating for sexual liberation in the 1960s and 1970s mark a continuation in the sense that they find their source and inspiration very largely in the Victorian age, especially the 1860s and 1870s.

Free love against marriage; Kate Millett against Norman Mailer; gay liberation against the cult of the heterosexual; ours is a period that includes at least as many conflicts as the Victorian. In a way, since it seems now more difficult to know which ideas really are what Shaw calls "advanced," since our political lexicon of liberal and conservative, radical and reactionary, revolutionary and counterrevolutionary has become much less useful, our age includes more conflict and confusion than the Victorian.

But, finally, we are not so far removed from the last century as we might like to think.

When the sex-obsessed Victorian age gave way to our own sex-obsessed age, it was partly for the better. But only partly. For one thing, no contemporary of ours can be considered as courageous as some of the great Victorians in responding to sexual repression, sexual injustice, intolerance, and hypocrisy. Mill, Eliot, Meredith, even in his own way Swinburne, and at last, Shaw—all were thought to approve or openly to practice living in sin.

Notes on Sources

CHAPTER 1—The Century That Discovered Sex

The two most recent, and best, books on Victoria are by Elizabeth Longford—*Queen Victoria: Born to Succeed* (1964) —and by Cecil Woodham-Smith—*Queen Victoria: From Her Birth to the Death of the Prince Consort* (1972). The Longford book has a good deal about John Brown.

Walter Houghton's *Victorian Frame of Mind* (1957) has a chapter, "Love," with sections on "Woman," "Sex," and "Love" itself. Attitudes toward sex (mostly nervous) on the part of Charlotte Brontë, Matthew Arnold, and a number of other Victorians are cited in the section on that subject. Houghton also cites Clarence Decker's *The Victorian Conscience* (1952), a book which is mostly about horrified Victorian reactions to French novels, specifically to the novels of Émile Zola.

Hippolyte Taine's observations on the number of prostitutes in London, and on other social matters, are included in his *Notes sur l'Angleterre*—in English, *Notes on England* (1871, 1872).

The book by Steven Marcus is *The Other Victorians: A Study of Sexuality and Pornography in Mid-Nineteenth-Century England* (1964). It is concerned, for the most part, with underground art and literature.

The story of the sex scandal that destroyed Sir Charles Dilke's career has been given in various forms. One is a play, *The Right Honorable Gentleman,* that had a successful run in London and a moderately successful one in New York. The fullest and best account is that of Roy Jenkins in his book *Sir Charles Dilke: A Victorian Tragedy* (1965), which was published in the United States as *Victorian Scandal.*

CHAPTER 2—Victorian Rebels

J. C. Reid, in *The Mind and Art of Coventry Patmore* (1957), comments on Patmore's relating of sex and religion. He also gives an account of the writer's life. The best edition of Patmore is that done by Frederick Page (1949).

The modern Anglo-Catholic scholar who writes about Patmore's glorifying of uncompleted sexual intercourse is Hoxie Neale Fairchild:

> Remembering Patmore's fondness for using Scriptural phrases like "Consummatum est" in a private erotic sense, "He who leaves all for my sake" might conceivably mean, "He who engages in sexual intercourse but withdraws from it before its climax."
>
> •   •   •   •
>
> But one hesitates to believe that the deepest secret of Patmore's esterocism was anything so shabby as *coitus interruptus.*
>
> *Religious Trends in English Poetry,*
> IV (New York, 1957), 344.

Although Professor Fairchild's analysis of Patmore's peculiar sexual doctrine is brilliant, it is tempting to add that, all things considered, the word *conceivably* seems ironic—no one was going to conceive if the husband withdrew before ejaculation!—and that while Fairchild may hesitate to believe what he himself has tended to prove, he never denies it.

The idea that Victorians translated the "Fall of Man" into the "Fall of Woman" as a virtually mythic theme was suggested to me by Rosalie Glynn Grylls (Lady Mander), author of books and essays about Shelley, Rossetti, and other nineteenth-century artists.

The story of the Mill-Taylor triangle is told in F. A. Hayek's *John Stuart Mill and Harriet Taylor* (1951). In this book, Mill's 1832 essay on marriage is published for the first time; its radicalism, which seems tame now, prevented its appearing until some hundred and twenty years after it was written!

The fullest account of Mill's life as a whole and of his ideas about sex, women, and marriage is the biography by Michael St. John Packe, *The Life of John Stuart Mill* (1954); here, the events in the Mill-Taylor relationship are recounted at some length.

Henry Taylor in his *Autobiography* (1885) describes the manners and looks of the young Mill (I, 78). (He was not related to John Taylor, Harriet's husband.)

"A Crisis in My Mental History: One Stage Onward" is Chapter Five in Mill's own *Autobiography,* published after his death (1873). This chapter, which is the heart of the work, shows the young Mill moving away from the cold intellectual influence of his father and toward the warm emotional influence of Harriet; and it describes the author's depression and virtual nervous breakdown.

The remark about a passion that "sprang out of the bushes" when the young Mill and Harriet Taylor met comes, again, from Henry Taylor—from a letter included in his published *Correspondence,* edited by Edward Dowden (1888, pages 326–327).

Carlyle's description of Harriet as a "romance heroine" is quoted in Hayek's book (page 80). Hayek also quotes Harriet at length—from her unpublished essay and from her letters—on the subject of marriage.

The best brief telling of the Fox-Flower story, that affair that seems so un-Victorian, is in Packe's biography of Mill. Packe also gives an account of the Bullers' party and of Roebuck's break with Mill.

Betty Miller's study, *Robert Browning: A Portrait* (1952) makes the reference to Browning's father; its main interest, however, is in Browning's relationships with his mother and his wife. This book argues that, for better or worse, the poet was in-

fluenced by Elizabeth Barrett Browning to abandon his Shel-
leyan Romanticism and independence and to appear, at least,
religiously orthodox. The implication is clear that Browning
more or less consciously resented his wife's influence—even while
he gave way to it—because Elizabeth replaced his mother as an
authoritative figure.

A more sympathetic, more thorough, and less readable
biography is Maisie Ward's, in two volumes, *Robert Browning
and His World: The Private Face* (1967) and *Robert Browning
and His World: Two Robert Brownings?* (1969).

The best combination of Browning criticism and Browning
biography is a book begun by William Irvine and completed,
after Irvine's death, by Park Honan: *The Ring, The Book and
The Poet* (1974), which focuses on Browning's masterpiece but
includes as well a good deal about the man himself.

William C. DeVane's account of the poet's life in the still
indispensable *Browning Handbook* (2nd edition, 1955) is relatively brief but very helpful; this classic handbook gives explana-
tory comments on all of Browning's poems. The letter quoted,
written by Edward FitzGerald, is a good example of how DeVane
fills in relevant background for even Browning's minor verse.

The *Works* of George Meredith (1910) include three volumes of poetry (XXIV, XXV, and XXVI) and twenty-six volumes of prose. A fuller and more accurate edition of Meredith, a
result of many years' labor by the late Phyllis Bartlett, is forth-
coming.

The fullest and best biography of Meredith is Lionel Stevenson's *The Ordeal of George Meredith* (1953); and many of the
facts about his life that are dealt with briefly here have been
drawn from that source.

Diane Johnson's *Lesser Lives* (1972)—its full title is *The
True History of the First Mrs. Meredith and Other Lesser Lives*
—gives the most complete account of Meredith's disastrous first
marriage, with emphasis on Mary Ellen Peacock Nicolls Meredith.

For Thomas Hardy, the standard biography is that produced
by the dean of American Hardy scholars, Carl J. Weber. It is

Hardy of Wessex: His Life and Literary Career (revised edition, 1965) —although the "official" Hardy biography is *Life* by F. E. Hardy (1962). Probably the best and most useful critical study is Irving Howe's *Thomas Hardy* (1968).

On Victorian reactions to French novelists, and in particular to Émile Zola, the usual source is Clarence Decker's *The Victorian Conscience* (1952).

CHAPTER 3—Victorian Triangles

The best introduction to John Ruskin's life and work for the modern reader is John Rosenberg's *The Darkening Glass: A Portrait of Ruskin's Genius* (1963). But this is not primarily a biography. Another worthwhile study is *John Ruskin* by Joan Evans (1954).

The inside story of the Ruskin-Effie Gray-John Everett Millais triangle is told by Sir William James in *The Order of Release* (1947).

Ruskin's autobiography, *Praeterita,* in which he recalls the young Rose La Touche, now appears to be largely fabricated, a fantasy more than an account of facts—although this probably does not apply to his memories of Rose.

Gordon Haight's *George Eliot: A Biography* (1968) is the fullest and most reliable account of the author's life, although the authorized biography of 1885 by John Cross (her husband for the last months of her life) is still of some interest: this is the three-volume *George Eliot's Life as Related to Her Letters and Journals.*

The comment on Ruskin's benign version of "Victorian sexual myth" is from Kate Millett's *Sexual Politics* (1970), which contrasts Ruskin not with George Eliot but with John Stuart Mill.

Herbert Spencer's *Autobiography* (two volumes, 1904) reveals his humorless and obtuse qualities along with (rather simple-minded) intellectual seriousness that may have had *some* appeal for the earnest young writer-to-be, George Eliot.

Unfortunately, there is no satisfactory modern edition of

George Eliot's work that is even approximately complete. The most useful text, still, is the twelve-volume Warwick edition (1901–1903).

Charles Dickens has been somewhat better served by twentieth-century editors than George Eliot. The Nonesuch edition of his work, in twenty-three volumes (1937–1938), is not comprehensive—Dickens wrote an astonishing amount, much of it anonymous—but this set is handsome, readable, and probably as accurate as any one can find.

The standard biography of Dickens is that by Edgar Johnson, subtitled *His Tragedy and Triumph* (2 volumes, 1952); this is a work of literary criticism as well as a life. Probably its main value, however, *is* biographical. Virtually all the given facts and quotations about the author's career, marriage, and extramarital affair come from these volumes.

The most complete life of Dante Gabriel Rossetti is Oswald Doughty's *A Victorian Romantic* (1949; revised edition, 1960). Some readers have thought Doughty's treatment biased. To correct this supposed bias, Rosalie Glynn Grylls has written a biography that is much more sympathetic to Rossetti: *Portrait of Rossetti* (1964).

Henry James's enthusiastic description of Janey Morris, written in a letter to his sister, is quoted by Doughty early in the fifth chapter of his Part III; but James changed his mind about the lady—and her circle—in later years. He tended to become increasingly cold to what he thought of as the Bohemianism of the aging pre-Raphaelites.

Philip Henderson's *William Morris* (1967) deals with the artist-writer's views on sex and marriage and with the difficulty of his position in the Rossetti-Morris triangle.

Both Rossetti and Morris represent, again, examples of how nineteenth-century English writers have been neglected by modern editors; there is no complete scholarly edition of either. For Morris, one has to rely on the twenty-four volume set edited by his daughter May (1910–1915). For Rossetti, the only more or less complete source—of his poetry only—is the edition (published in both one- and two-volume versions) produced by his brother, William Michael Rossetti (1911).

CHAPTER 4—Victorian Deviants

There is no complete and completely satisfactory life of Algernon Swinburne. Biographies by Samuel C. Chew (1929) and Georges Lafourcade (1932) are solid and useful; but basic revelations about the poet have emerged in the past three decades— including the fact that Swinburne's first and great love was his cousin Mary Gordon Leith, the author of the earliest personal memoirs that deal with the poet. The *Life* by Edmund Gosse (1917), once supposed to be standard and reliable, is now virtually useless; it became one of twenty volumes in the Bonchurch edition of Swinburne (1925–1927), edited by Edmund Gosse and by T. J. Wise, who has since been shown to be a forger of editions (*his* biography is entitled *Forging Ahead*). Unfortunately for students, the dubious Bonchurch edition is almost the only source for most of Swinburne's prose. For his poetry, the greatly preferable source is the six-volume set originally published by Chatto in 1904 and reprinted a number of times by Heinemann.

The best brief critical account of Swinburne's poetry is by John Rosenberg in the introduction to his excellent selection of the author's *Poetry and Prose* (1968).

For a sense of Swinburne's odd and complex personality, and, above all, for an insight into his fascination with sadism and masochism, the best source may well be Cecil Y. Lang's edition, in six volumes, of *The Swinburne Letters* (1959–1962).

Swinburne's prose fiction is fragmentary but extensive and revealing. Probably the best-known edition of these is *The Novels of A. C. Swinburne: Love's Cross Currents; Lesbia Brandon* (1962). But this confusing and unscholarly version, edited and introduced by the aging, crotchety Edmund Wilson, is less reliable than the pioneer work on which it relies, the Randolph Hughes edition published under the simple title *Lesbia Brandon* (1952). (Hughes himself, in his introduction and notes, is odd and crotchety, but his work is full and mostly accurate.) That title, not incidentally, is one that Swinburne never gave to his fiction-in-manuscript about aristocratic family life, sexual intrigue, masochism, and incest.

A recent and lively account of Swinburne's later years is the book by Mollie Panter-Downes, *At the Pines: Swinburne and Watts-Dunton in Putney* (1971).

The most complete account of the life of Monckton Milnes is James Pope Hennessy's biography in two volumes (1940, 1951).

Fawn M. Brodie's *The Devil Drives: A Life of Sir Richard Burton* (1967) is the latest and most candid biography of the explorer. Most of my information comes directly from this source. Although Burton's translation of the *Thousand and One Nights* (1885) —generally known simply as the *Arabian Nights*—is by far his best-known work (and his introduction and notes to it, especially those on sexual customs, are still fascinating), Burton was an indefatigable writer, turning out nearly fifty separate publications in his lifetime.

A valuable source for the life and work of Simeon Solomon is William E. Fredeman's *Pre-Raphaelitism: A Bibliocritical Study* (1965), which cites all of the sources for our knowledge of the fascinating but still obscure artist. I am grateful to Mr. Robert Isaacson of New York for allowing me to transcribe a copy of the jury's indictment of Solomon on a charge of sexual misbehavior in a public place.

The fullest biography of Oscar Wilde is by Hesketh Pearson: *The Life of Wilde* (1946). Recent critical books on Wilde are likely to be, like Edouard Roditi's (1947), irrationally hostile, or, like George Woodcock's (1949), inconclusive—although Woodcock's *Paradox of Oscar Wilde* is certainly more worthwhile than Roditi's shallow book.

The Rupert Hart-Davis edition of Wilde's letters (1962) is a very thorough, scholarly one; its contents are revealing and sometimes moving.

CHAPTER 5—An End and Some Beginnings

Arnold's attack on John Roebuck and other smug Victorian optimists occurs in his famous essay, "The Function of Criticism at the Present Time," which is one part of his 1865 *Essays in Criticism.*

A biased but amusing account of the Ruskin-Whistler controversy and lawsuit is given by Whistler himself in that collec-

tion of essays and comments entitled—with dandyish irony—
The Gentle Art of Making Enemies.

Much of the material included here on the sexual roles assumed by men and women in the England of the nineteenth
century is touched upon—and sometimes treated more fully—in
my book *Sex and Marriage in Victorian Poetry* (1975); as the
title indicates, however, that book is a good deal more limited in
scope than this one.

Michael Pearson's *The Five Pound Virgins,* published first
in England as *The Age of Consent: Victorian Prostitution and
Its Enemies* (1972), gives the fullest report yet—going beyond
nineteenth-century statistical and sociological documents—of its
subject.

Michael Holroyd's two-volume biography, *Lytton Strachey,*
is recent and apparently complete; it certainly makes no bones
about, for instance, Strachey's homosexuality. The two volumes,
published separately, are *The Unknown Years—1880–1910* (1967)
and *The Years of Achievement—1910–1932* (1968).

Probably the best source for Norman Mailer's considered
ideas on sex and the sexes is his *Prisoner of Sex* (1971); here
Mailer, who is frank in revealing his prejudices and his passions, seems alternately attractive for his candor and repellent
for his sexual narrowness and what one has at last to call failed
mysticism.

Index